ANCIENT CIVILIZATIONS

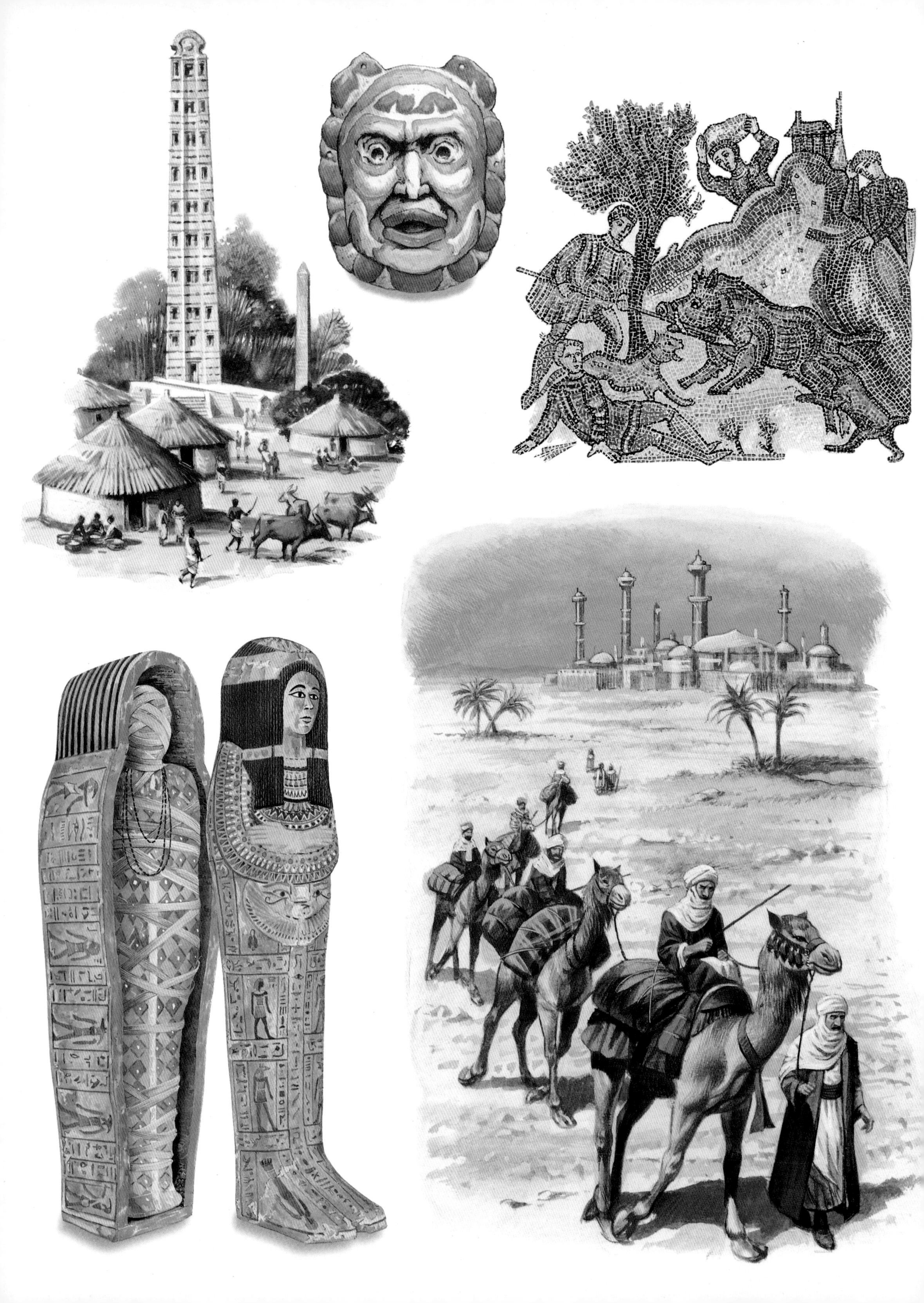

ANCIENT CIVILIZATIONS

HOW PEOPLE LIVED AROUND THE WORLD AND THROUGH THE AGES

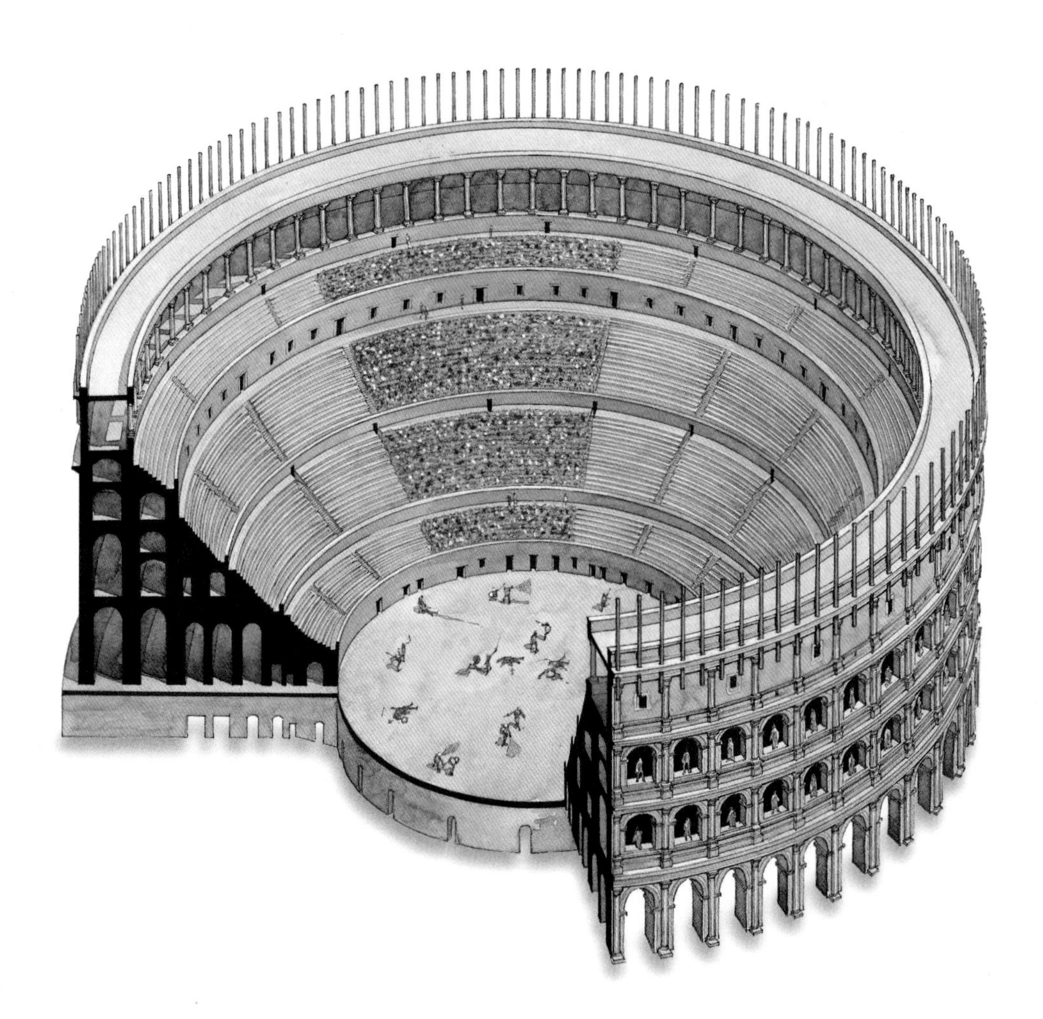

PHILIP BROOKS

This edition is published by Armadillo, an imprint of Anness Publishing Ltd,
108 Great Russell Street, London WC1B 3NA; info@anness.com

www.armadillobooks.co.uk; www.annesspublishing.com; twitter: @Anness_Books

Anness Publishing has a new picture agency outlet for images for publishing, promotions or advertising. Please visit our website www.practicalpictures.com for more information.

A CIP catalogue record for this book is available from the British Library

Publisher: Joanna Lorenz
Produced by Miles Kelly Publishing Limited
Project Editor: Raje Airey
Design: Casebourne Rose Associates

PICTURE CREDITS
The publishers would like to thank the following artists who have contributed to this book:
Mark Beesley; Richard Berridge (Spec Art); Vanessa Card; James Field (SGA); Wayne Ford; Terry Gabbey; Gary Hincks; Sally Holmes; Richard Hook (Linden Artists); John James (Temple Rogers); Steve Lings (Linden Artists); Shane Marsh (Linden Artists); Rob McCaig; Alex Pang (SGA); Terry Riley; Chris Rothero (Linden Artists); Eric Rowe (Linden Artists); Martin Sanders; Peter Sarson; Rob Sheffield; Don Simpson (Spec Art); Roger Stewart; Ken Stott; Mike Taylor (SGA); Mike White (Temple Rogers).
Maps: Stuart Squires and Steve Sweet (SGA).

The publishers wish to thank the following for supplying photographs for this book:
Page 13 (B/L) Erich Lessing/AKG London; 19 (T/L) Paul Almasy/AKG London; 22 (B/R) Jean-Louis Nou/AKG Berlin; 40 (T/R) Mary Evans Picture Library; 49 (T/L) iStock; 53 (T/L) AKG London.

All other photographs from Dover Publications and Miles Kelly Archives

PUBLISHER'S NOTE
Although the information in this book is believed to be accurate and true at the time of going to press, neither the authors nor the publisher can accept any legal responsibility or liability for any errors or omissions that may have been made.

Manufacturer: Anness Publishing Ltd,
108 Great Russell Street, London WC1B 3NA, England
For Product Tracking go to: www.annesspublishing.com/tracking
Batch: 7470-23638-1127

Contents

Introduction

▲ BUILDINGS
The magnificent royal palace of Persepolis was built in ancient Persia's greatest city to reflect power and wealth.

▼ TIMELINE
The civilizations of the ancient world cover a vast time span of about 4500 years: from the first cities of Sumer to the later kingdoms based in Africa.

WHAT IS A CIVILIZATION? The term comes from the Latin word, *civis*, which means "citizen of a city". So a civilization is a group of people living together in a large town or city, who have developed a culture – a way of life with its own special quality.

There are several key ingredients in a civilized culture. An early civilization may not have all of them, but it will certainly have some. They include writing, a system of government, organized religion and the ability to construct buildings and monuments on a grand scale. This section of the book describes some ancient cultures that developed along these lines.

Most of the features of civilization began to develop thousands of years ago during the Stone Age. But it took a long time for people to bring all these ideas together and to build cities on a large scale. This happened at different times in different parts of the world, as is shown on the Timeline below.

No one knows why civilizations occurred in some parts of the world much earlier than others. But cities can only grow when the food supply is reliable enough to supply the town-dwellers, who have no way of growing their own food. People had to develop

▲ RELIGION
This stone carving from the Indus Valley civilization may have been a god or a king. As far as we know, all ancient civilizations had some form of organized religion.

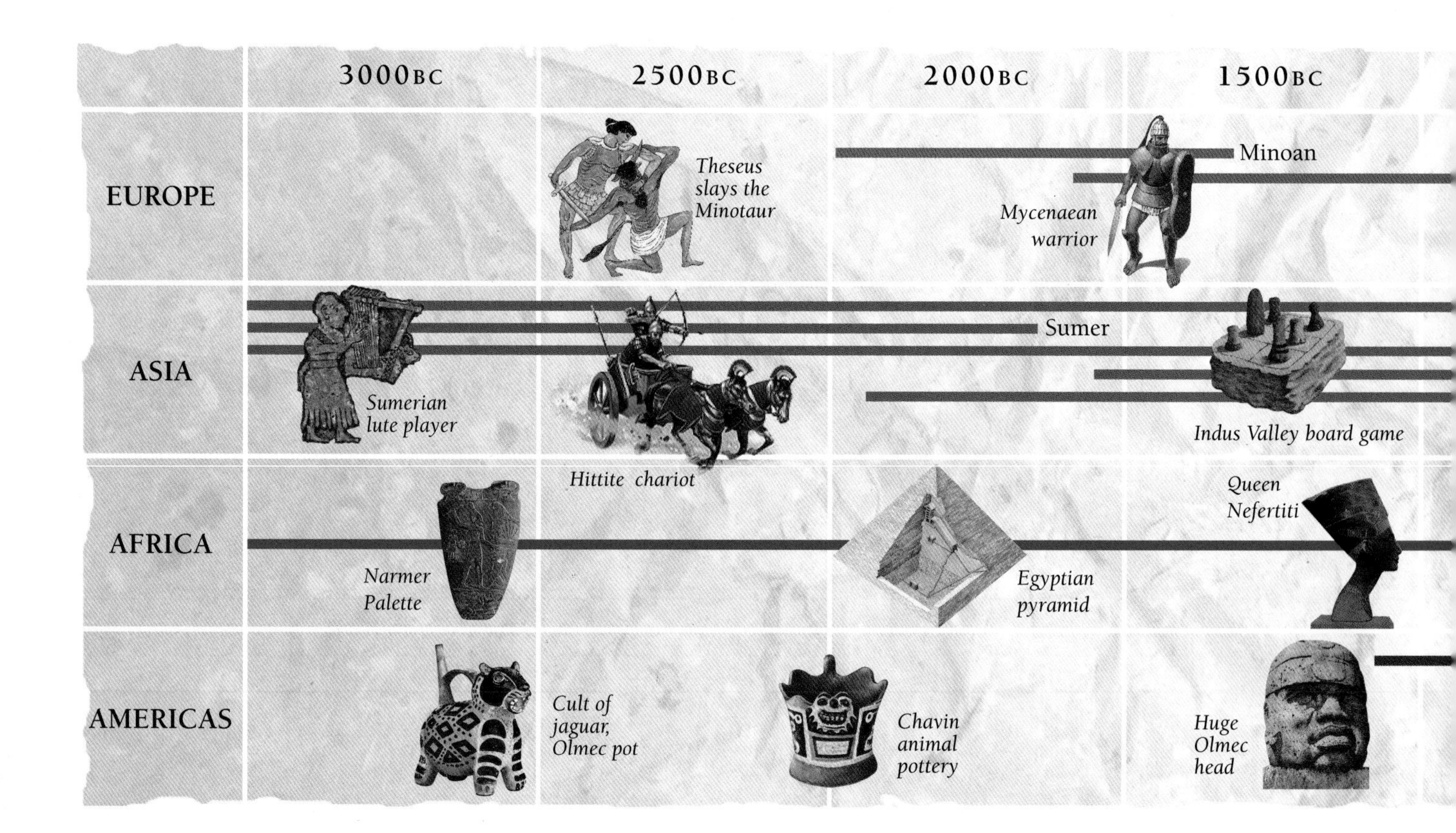

▲ WRITING
The marks on this ancient bone are the earliest examples of Chinese script. Writing is a key feature of a civilization.

▶ TRADE
The Romans traded in ships such as this. As civilizations developed and produced a surplus of goods, they set up trading links with others.

efficient farming, and ways of storing and trading food, before they could build large cities. Trade in food also provided a network for trading the products of city workshops – items made of pottery, metal, and wood which city people sold.

Many ancient civilizations built up large empires, either by conquering other settlements in battle or by building up trade networks which allowed them to dominate the surrounding peoples. This meant that many ancient cultures became rich, and their power spread over a large area of the globe. The Roman empire and the empire of Alexander the Great are two examples.

Civilizations such as these have left large amounts of evidence behind them. Archaeologists – people who study the remains of cultures – are still digging up artefacts made by craft workers thousands of years ago. Complex funeral customs, as in ancient Egypt, can tell us a great deal about the civilization. Together with ancient documents and the remains of ancient cities, these things provide a fascinating glimpse of how life was lived thousands of years ago.

▲ FARMING
A civilization can only develop when its food supply is secure and the growing of crops is not left to chance. Evidence shows that rice was cultivated in China around 5000BC. Rice farming arrived in Japan in about 200BC.

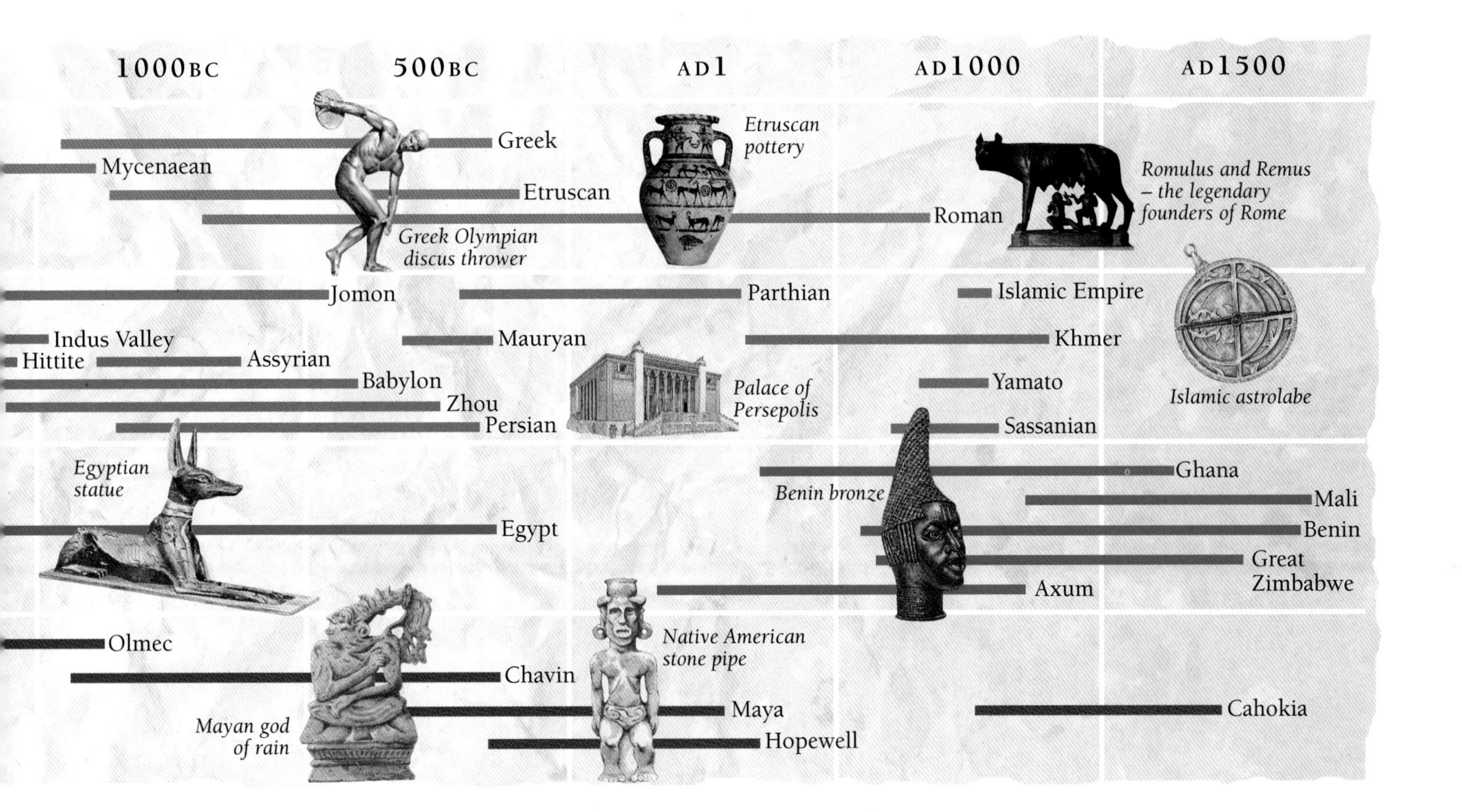

The Sumerians

HOME TO THOUSANDS of people and bustling with activity, the world's first cities were built in Mesopotamia, the land between the Tigris and Euphrates rivers in what is now Iraq. The narrow streets and whitewashed mud-brick houses of cities such as Uruk and Ur were home to craftworkers who made pottery and metalwork that were traded as far afield as Arabia and India. People from the region made the world's first wheeled carts and chariots, and invented the world's first known writing system, called "cuneiform" script. For these reasons, Mesopotamia became known as "the cradle of civilization".

One group of people to settle in Mesopotamia were the Sumerians. They arrived in Sumer, the southern part of the area, in about 5000BC. The climate was hot and dry but farmers learned to use water from the rivers to irrigate their fields and grow plentiful crops of wheat, barley, dates and vegetables.

The Sumerians' first city was Uruk, which they built by the River Euphrates. By 3500BC, some 10,000 people lived there. The winding streets of the city surrounded its biggest building, the temple of Anu, the greatest of the Sumerians' many gods. Here the priests worshipped Anu in the hope that he would bring good weather and rich harvests. The people, who knew that they would starve if the harvests were poor, brought generous offerings to the temple. This made the priests some of the richest, most powerful people in the city.

Soon, other cities were founded all over Mesopotamia. They were similar to Uruk, with large temples, called ziggurats, and mud-brick houses. Each city was independent, with its own ruler, priests and merchants. As the cities grew rich from their trade, they competed with each other for power over the whole region.

The Sumerian cities remained independent until about 2350BC. Then the Akkadians, from an area north of Sumer, conquered the area and made it part of their large Mesopotamian empire.

▶ PLOUGH
Sumerian farmers developed the ox-drawn plough in about 4000BC. It was much more efficient than a hand-held plough and meant that they could grow a great deal more food.

FERTILE LAND
Separate city states made up the Sumerian civilization but there were similarities between them. Each used the Tigris and Euphrates for trade and transport and all had mud-brick buildings. Also, they relied on fertile farmland to produce food. The region was so fertile, it is often called the Fertile Crescent.

◀ LUTE PLAYER
Musicians playing lutes, pipes and tambourines, provided entertainment while people banqueted, drank beer, and watched celebrations. The people of Ur enjoyed music at home and at great festivals such as New Year.

▶ GRAVE GOODS
Gold items, such as adornments, were placed in the tombs of the early kings and queens of Ur. Servants followed their king or queen to the grave. After a royal death, the servants walked into the huge tomb, drank poison, and lay down to die next to the body of their royal master or mistress.

▲ STANDARD OF UR
Pictures made from shells and precious stones show a row of Sumerian farmers herding cattle and sheep. Below them, workers carry heavy loads. These pictures, known as the Standard of Ur, may once have decorated a Sumerian musical instrument.

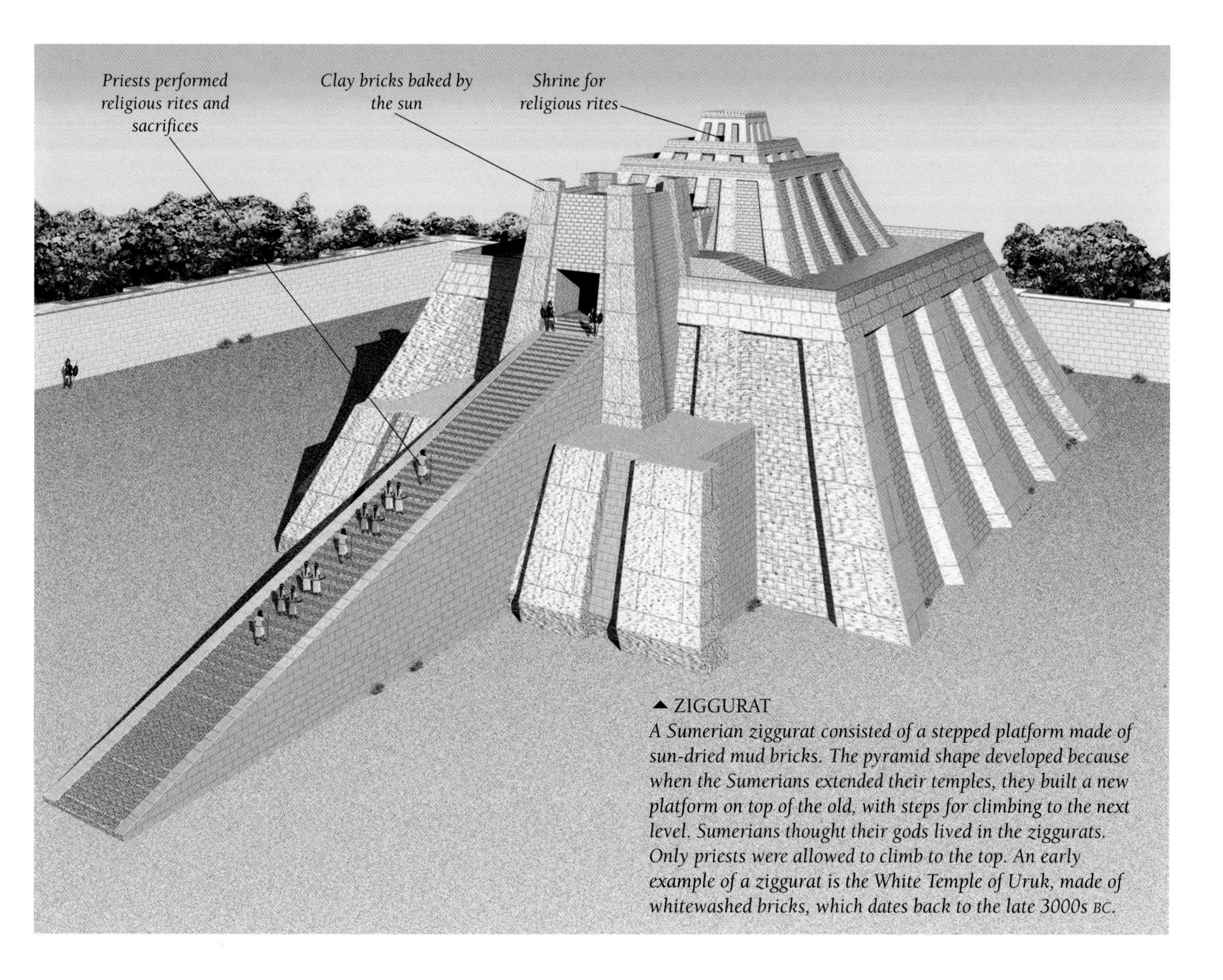

▲ ZIGGURAT
A Sumerian ziggurat consisted of a stepped platform made of sun-dried mud bricks. The pyramid shape developed because when the Sumerians extended their temples, they built a new platform on top of the old, with steps for climbing to the next level. Sumerians thought their gods lived in the ziggurats. Only priests were allowed to climb to the top. An early example of a ziggurat is the White Temple of Uruk, made of whitewashed bricks, which dates back to the late 3000s BC.

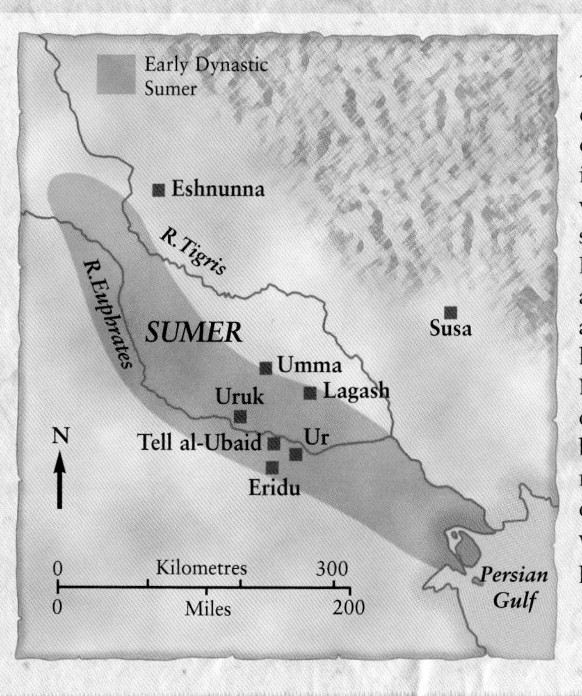

◀ SUMER
The Sumerian civilization consisted of independent, walled city states such as Ur, Lagash, Umma and Uruk. It arose in the area known as Mesopotamia, or "the land between two rivers", which covered much of what is now present-day Iraq.

Key Dates

- 5000BC The Sumerians, a farming people, settle in southern Mesopotamia.
- 4000BC Ox-drawn plough introduced.
- 3500BC Uruk becomes one of the world's first cities. Sumerians develop the potter's wheel and wheeled transport.
- 2900BC Earliest known writing.
- 2500BC Ur becomes a major city.
- 2350BC King Sargon from Akkad conquers the area of Sumer.
- 2100BC Ur is the most important Mesopotamian city, under King Ur-Nammu.
- 1700BC Ur declines, and the city of Babylon gains in strength.

Ancient Babylon

▲ CLAY LION
A clay lion which stood guard outside one of the Babylonian temples. Its intricate detail shows that the Babylonians were skilled sculptors. The lion was a popular symbol of royal power.

AROUND 1900BC, the Amorites, a people from Syria, moved into Mesopotamia, the land between the Tigris and Euphrates rivers. They farmed barley, herded sheep and goats and were skilled in all sorts of crafts, from metal working to perfumery and from leather making to beekeeping.

The Amorites made their capital at the city of Babylon, by the Euphrates. During the late 1700s BC, their king Hammurabi conquered the whole of southern Mesopotamia, which became known as Babylonia. The conquered land contained peoples of many different cultures and laws, so Hammurabi decided to unify the laws. They were inscribed on a stone stela, or tablet, for all to see.

Under Hammurabi, Babylon became a great area of science and learning. Babylonian scholars developed a numbering system, based on groups of 60, which is how we get our 60-minute hour and 360-degree circle. The scientists of Babylon were also renowned astronomers, recording the movements of the moon and stars across the night sky.

The rulers of many nearby cultures were jealous of Babylon's power and the wealth the Babylonians earned from trade, and so the city was attacked many times. Hittites, from the area that is now Turkey, raided Babylon, then Kassites, from mountains to the east, invaded and took over the city. They turned Babylon into an important religious area, with a large temple to the supreme god, Marduk.

▶ ISHTAR GATE
The Ishtar Gate, decorated with spectacular blue stone, straddled the Processional Way which led into the city of Babylon. Three walls ringed the city, each so thick that two chariots could drive side by side along the top.

SCIENCE AND LAW

Babylon was a sophisticated city and a focal point for science, literature and learning. Scholars studied mathematics and astronomy, the science of the stars. Their ideas continue to influence us today.

◀ THE LAWS OF HAMMURABI
Hammurabi's laws were carved into a stela of black basalt rock. They include laws about money, property, the family and the rights of slaves. According to the law, a wrongdoer had to be punished in a way that suited the crime. The phrase "an eye for an eye and a tooth for a tooth" originates from Hammurabi's laws.

▲ MAP OF THE WORLD
A stone map showing the known land masses surrounded by a ring of ocean. The map was made by Babylonian scholars more than 3,000 years ago. They marked it with wedge-shaped cuneiform writing.

◀ HANGING GARDENS
King Nebuchadnezzar built fabulous hanging, or terraced, gardens for his wife Amytis to remind her of the green hill country of her home in Media. One of the ancient world's great wonders, no one today really knows what the gardens looked like.

▼ DRAGON OF MARDUK
The dragon symbolized Marduk, supreme god of the Babylonians. The Babylonians worshipped many gods. They included the sun god, Shamash, and Ishtar, goddess of war and love.

In around 900BC, the Chaldeans, horsemen from the Gulf coast, invaded Babylon. Their greatest king, Nebuchadnezzar II, rebuilt the city more magnificently than before. He gave it massive mud-brick walls, strong gates and a seven-floor ziggurat. He also built a palace for himself and the Hanging Gardens, which was one of the Seven Wonders of the ancient world.

Babylon became the largest city in western Asia. Trade along the rivers, and via the caravan routes leading eastward to Iran, also made it wealthy once more. Its magnificence survived until it was again invaded, this time by the Persians.

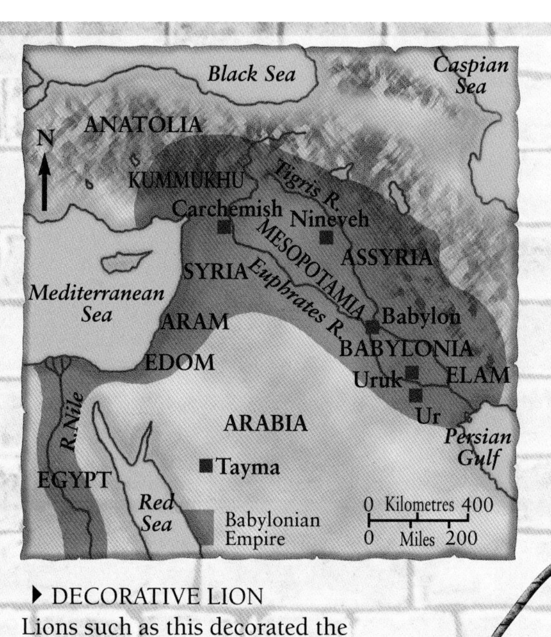

◀ BABYLON
The map shows the extent of the Babylonian empire in the 7th century BC. It was small compared with other ancient kingdoms, but contained some of the most advanced cities of the period. These included Ur, Uruk and Babylon, the empire's capital.

▶ DECORATIVE LION
Lions such as this decorated the Ishtar Gate. The gate was named after the Babylonian goddess, Ishtar.

Key Dates

- 1900BC Babylon becomes the chief city of the Amorites.
- 1792–1750BC Reign of King Hammurabi, law-giver and conqueror of Mesopotamia.
- 1595–1155BC The Kassites rule the city of Babylon.
- 900BC The Chaldeans take over Babylon and begin to rebuild it.
- 605–562BC Reign of King Nebuchadnezzar. He builds the fabulous Hanging Gardens. Babylon is the most sophisticated city in the Near East.

The Hittites

▲ PRISONER
Egyptian mosaic tile, dating from c.1170BC, shows a Hittite prisoner.

FROM THE COLD, mountainous region of central Anatolia (modern Turkey) came the Hittites, powerful peoples who flourished between about 1600 and 1200BC. A warlike group, they battled constantly with nearby settlements for control over Mediterranean trade.

The Hittites had to master a harsh homeland, finding lands to farm wheat and barley and raise sheep and cattle. They built a huge stronghold at Hattusas, in the heart of their kingdom. From here, they recruited and trained a powerful army. They were among the first to use horses in warfare and developed the chariot as one of the most feared weapons of battle.

They attacked the Mitanni, from northern Mesopotamia, and took over Syria. Their charioteers even threatened the power of the great Egyptian empire. The Hittites also used peaceful means to increase their power. They made treaties with the Egyptian pharaohs, which have been found in clay tablets in the massive royal archives at Hattusas. These show that the Hittites sometimes bought off their rivals with gold.

The Hittites had a strong land army but found it hard to defend their coasts. Invaders from the sea, known as the "Sea Peoples", attacked them constantly. This, together with bad harvests and pressure from Egypt, led to their downfall in around 1200BC.

◀ SOLDIER OR GOD?
No one knows for sure whether this armed man is a soldier or a Hittite god. He seems to be flexing his muscles. Placed at the gate of the city, he would have put fear into the hearts of any attacker.

▼ LION GATE
Fearsome-looking lions decorated the stone gateways of Hattusas, the Hittite capital and one of the strongest cities of its time. Set among cliffs and mountains, the city was well protected from enemies.

ARMIES
Both the Hittites and Assyrians had powerful armies but the Assyrian army was the most feared and efficient of its time. Consisting of foot soldiers and heavily armed cavalry, Assyrian armies were huge, several thousand strong. Many of the soldiers were captured people from lands that the Assyrians had conquered.

◀ CHARIOTEERS
Much of the Hittite military success came from their skill as charioteers. Their chariots, which could hold up to three people, one to drive the horses, and two to fight, were feared by all.

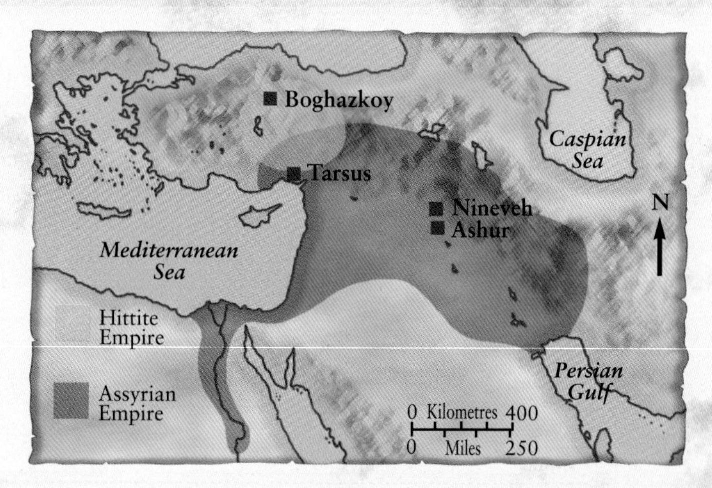

▲ HITTITES AND ASSYRIANS
The Hittites controlled much of modern Turkey and parts of northern Mesopotamia and Syria. Their real hub of power was around Hattusas and the cities of Alaca and Alisar. The Assyrian empire stretched from the Mediterranean to the Persian Gulf.

The Assyrians

THEY WERE THE MOST FEARED people of the ancient world. The armies of the Assyrians attacked swiftly, ransacking villages, battering down city walls, and killing anyone in the way. They carried away precious metals, timber, building stone – anything they could use. They took prisoners to work as slaves on building projects in their cities along the upper Tigris river – building luxurious palaces, towering temples, and massive city walls.

The Assyrians seemed unstoppable. They conquered an empire that stretched from the Nile Delta to the ancient cities of Babylon and Ur. They built beautiful cities, such as Nineveh, Nimrud and Khorsabad, which were among the most magnificent the world had ever seen. Their royal palaces were decorated with stone reliefs that portrayed the success and glory of their kings. The reliefs survive today and show us much about the Assyrian kings and their lives – their war triumphs, use of chariots and battering rams, victory celebrations, conquered people bringing them lavish tribute, and hunting scenes.

The main strength of the Assyrians was their army but as Assyria grew in size, the soldiers could not defend the whole empire at once. One conquered city could not defeat the Assyrians but when the people of Babylonia and Media joined forces they could win, and the vast Assyrian empire quickly crumbled.

▲ WINGED SPHINX
Massive carved stone sphinxes guarded city gates and palaces. Winged beasts, they had bull or lion bodies and human heads with long beards, like those worn by Assyrian kings. The Assyrians believed the monsters gave heavenly protection and warded off evil wrongdoers.

▼ THE ROYAL HUNT
Assyrian kings enjoyed hunting, particularly for lions, wildest of all creatures. They wanted their people to think their strength was god-like and often had themselves portrayed performing feats of incredible strength and bravery.

▲ COURT LIFE
A stone relief shows musicians with harps and flutes playing at the palace of Assurbanipal in Nineveh. Reliefs such as this tell us much about court life.

▼ BATTERING RAMS
Assyrian soldiers used a fearsome fighting machine, part battering ram, part tower, to attack and break through the walls of enemy cities. While the metal-tipped battering ram was driven against the walls, soldiers on the tower used picks to break them down.

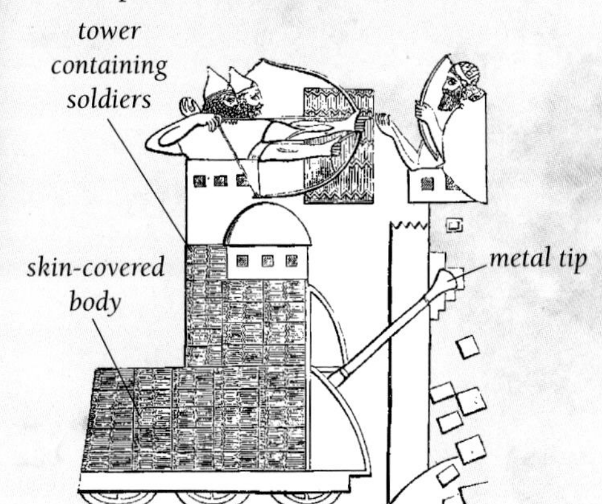

Key Dates

- c.2000BC Hittite farmers settle in Turkey.
- 1550BC Hattusas becomes Hittite capital.
- 1380–1346BC Hittites flourish.
- 1250BC Assyrians and Sea People attack Hittite empire.
- 1200BC Hittite empire declines.
- 883–859BC Nineveh built.
- 744–727BC Assyria reaches greatest power.
- 721–705BC King Sargon builds Assyrian capital, Khorsabad.
- 664BC Assyrians conquer Egypt.
- 612BC Nineveh destroyed.
- 609BC Babylonians defeat Assyrian army.

The Persian Empire

▲ PERSIAN SOLDIER
Mosaics of Persian soldiers decorated the palace of Susa. They were the keepers of law and order. An elite force of 10,000 warriors were called "immortals" because when one died, he was replaced immediately.

THEY BEGAN AS A SMALL nation from the region near Babylon. Suddenly, in around 549BC, the Persians seemed to be everywhere. Led by Cyrus the Great (r. 559–530BC), the Persian army pushed west and east, conquering a vast area that stretched from modern Turkey to the borders of India. Cyrus, and the emperors that followed him, gained enormous wealth from their conquests. They built cities with huge palaces, drank from gold and silver vessels, and surrounded themselves with luxury.

The Persian Empire was vast and mountainous and contained many different peoples, who often rebelled against Persian control. To keep order, the Persian rulers had a very effective army. Known as "the immortals", these 10,000 specially trained men were feared wherever they went and moved quickly to put down rebellions.

▲ TRIBUTES
Once a year representatives from the provinces came to the royal palace at Persepolis. Everyone brought gifts for the emperor – gold from India, horses from Assyria, two-humped camels from Bactria.

The emperors did not only rely on brute force. They also organized the empire so it could be controlled easily. They divided it into 20 provinces, each governed by a satrap, an official who ruled on behalf of the emperor. Each province raised taxes and tributes. The satraps were extremely powerful in their own right, so the emperor sent spies, known as "the king's ears", to each province to listen out for treachery and to check that the satraps were sending all the taxes to the emperor, not keeping some for themselves. The Persians also built a network of roads to link the corners of their empire. Spies, tax collectors and traders could travel easily around the countryside.

KING OF KINGS

Cyrus the Great belonged to the Achaemenid dynasty. He, and the Persian emperors who followed him, gave themselves the title King of Kings. They lived in grandeur and had absolute power. Below them, and their nobles, most of the population were farmers, craftworkers, serfs and slaves.

▸ SILVER GOAT
A silver ornament in the shape of a goat from the royal city of Persepolis. The Persians loved animals and used many different creatures to decorate all sorts of objects.

▲ DARIUS THE GREAT
Emperor Darius I ruled the Persian Empire from 522 to 486BC. He was head of the army and a wise ruler. He also founded Persepolis. During his reign, the empire reached its greatest extent.

▼ PERSIAN NOBLES
A Persian nobleman stands between two soldiers. Nobles were wealthy and educated. Darius appointed his satraps, or provincial governors, from noble-born families.

▼ PERSEPOLIS
The massive audience hall in the palace of Persepolis. The emperors, Darius I and Xerxes built a magnificent palace at the city of Persepolis. The huge staircase leading up to the audience hall was so wide that 8 horses could ride up it side by side. People came from all over the empire to pay tribute to the emperor who sat on his throne at the far side of the hall.

The Persians' wealth grew and the emperors brought skilled workers from all over the empire to build cities and palaces. Stone masons came from Greece, brickmakers from Babylon and goldsmiths from Egypt. The Persians also imported raw materials such as cedar wood from the Lebanon and ivory from Ethiopia.

Some people did fight off Persian invasions. The Scythians, fearless horsemen from the north, held back Persia's army, and the Greeks fought off two invasion attempts. The Greeks hated the Persians and eventually Alexander the Great, the famous conqueror from the Greek world, destroyed the Persian empire in 333BC.

▲ THE PERSIAN EMPIRE
The map shows the Persian Empire at its greatest extent in about 518BC. By then, Persia was the largest empire that the world had seen. It stretched from India to the Mediterranean. Susa was the capital. The empire included areas that had previously produced great civilizations: Egypt, Sumer, the Indus Valley and Anatolia.

Key Dates

- 835BC The Medes, from Media, southwest of the Caspian Sea, rule much of Iran.
- 549BC Cyrus becomes leader of the Persians. He conquers Media, Ionia and Lydia, so creating the first Persian empire.
- 522–486BC Reign of Darius I.
- 518BC Darius conquers parts of Egypt.
- 513BC Darius takes over the Indus Valley area.
- 490BC Persians invade Greece but are defeated at the Battle of Marathon.
- 480BC Xerxes leads another attempted invasion of Greece.
- 330BC Persia becomes part of the empire of Alexander the Great.

Parthians and Sassanians

CONQUERED BY THE GREAT Macedonian leader, Alexander the Great, the Persian empire ceased to exist. But after Alexander's death in 332BC, Persian leaders began again to take control of their native land. Once more they created a large empire, uniting diverse people, from sheep-herders in Iran to Mesopotamian farmers, under all-powerful emperors, whom they called the King of Kings.

Alexander, and the Achaemenid emperors before him, had shown the Persians that they needed a strong army to create a great empire. But the new Persian leaders, under two dynasties, the Parthians (240BC–AD226) and the more successful Sassanians (AD226–646), who replaced them, went further. They rebuilt society as a system of rigid social classes: nobles, priests, warriors, high and low officials, and peasants.

◀ PARTHIAN SHOT
Parthian cavalry pretended to retreat, then, unexpectedly, fired arrows backwards with deadly accuracy.

Everyone knew their place. People's whole lives, from the type of job they did to their choice of marriage partner, from how much tax they paid to the type of food they ate, all depended on the class to which they belonged.

This rigid class system kept the country united. At the top of the social tree, and sovereign ruler, was the emperor, the King of Kings himself. The people were reminded of his greatness, because the Sassanian emperors put their own images on everything they created. Their palaces and cites were decorated with stone reliefs and sculptures showing them in battle or enjoying sports such as hunting and horse riding.

▶ ROCK RELIEFS
Sassanian rulers recorded their achievements in stunning reliefs carved on the cliff faces of their native province of Fars. These show subjects such as Persian knights and Sassanian troops.

ZOROASTRIANISM

The Persians adopted Zoroastrianism as their religion. Zoroaster, or Zarathustra as he was also called, lived in about 1000BC. He taught that life was a fight between good and evil. Zoroastrians believed that the source of good in the world was the Wise Lord, a god of light and truth called Ahura Mazda. A sacred fire burned in every Persian temple as a symbol of his light and eternal goodness.

▶ AHURA MAZDA
The chief god of the Persians was Ahura Mazda, source of all goodness. A winged figure, he was the symbol of Zoroastrianism. Priests tended his sacred fire. They were called Magi, from which comes the word "magic".

▲ SACRED BULL
In ancient Persia, the bull was a symbol of power. The Persians also believed it was the first animal to be created and that, after the first bull was killed, all the other animals of the world were born from its soul.

▶ PARTHIAN AND SASSANIAN EMPIRES
The map shows the Parthian and Sassanian empires. They were not as vast as the first Persian empire but these later empires were still large. Parthian lands stretched from the farming area of Mesopotamia, north of the Persian Gulf, to the homelands of herders and nomads in central Iran. The domains of the later Sassians stretched still further east to the Indus River.

◄ CTESIPHON
The capital city, Ctesiphon, stood on the Tigris River, near to present-day Baghdad in Iraq. It grew dramatically in size during the Sassanian period, possibly containing several hundred thousand people. The Sassanians divided the city into two large suburbs. One part was for captives from the Roman empire, and the other was for the emperor and his family. The royal family lived in this large stone-built palace with its great vaulted central hall.

▲ STUCCO PANEL
Part of a decorative border from a Sassanian house. The upper classes loved luxury and their homes were decorated with ornate plasterwork, called stucco. This plasterwork was decorated with guinea fowl.

One of the most important classes was the priests. They were the leaders of the Zoroastrian religion. This faith had been developed in about 1000BC but the Sassanians made it the state religion, although contemporary eastern religions and other cults exerted an influence.

Under these later Persians, trade, industry and the arts flourished. They made developments in farming and improved irrigation systems. The local population rose but farmers worked the land too hard. Crops failed and the region became poor once more. Eventually, the Muslim Arabs invaded, finally ending the later Persian empires.

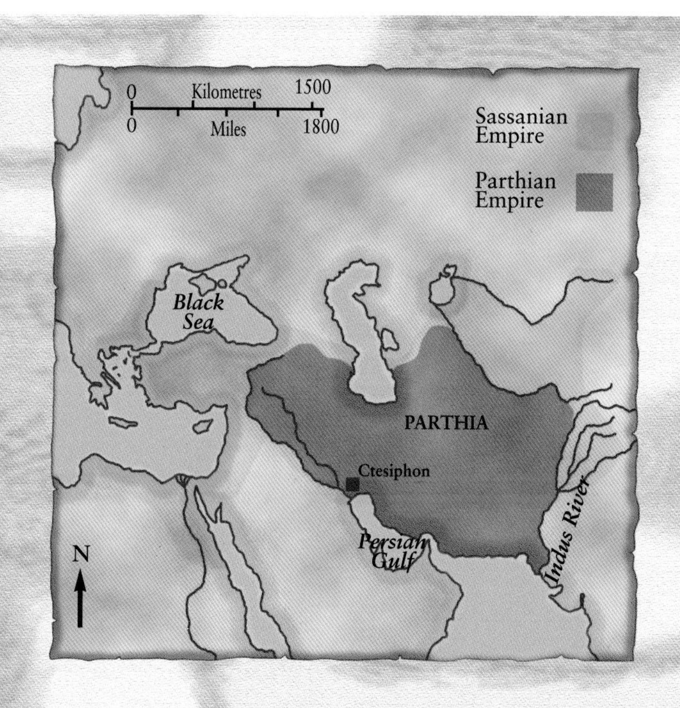

Key Dates

- c. 240BC–AD226 Parthian dynasty rules lands in Persia.
- AD109 Silk trade links China and Parthia.
- AD224 Ardashir, son of high priest Sasan destroys Parthian power. He founds Persian Sassian dynasty.
- AD226–642 Sassanian dynasty rules Persia.
- AD531–578 Reign of Khusrau Anushirvan. He reforms tax system and improves irrigation in Mesopotamia.
- AD614–628 Reign of Khusrau Parviz, conqueror of Egypt and Syria, the last of the great Sassanian kings.
- AD637 Muslim Arabs invade and destroy Sassanian Empire.

Islamic Empire

▲ MUSLIM WOMEN
Traditionally, many Muslim women cover their heads out of doors, and some wear clothes that cover them completely.

IN THE 7TH CENTURY AD, a new faith appeared that has become one of the world's greatest religions. It emerged in the Arabian peninsula, where the Arab people lived by farming and trading. They had worshipped many gods but in about AD610, the prophet Mohammed, a merchant from Mecca, announced that a new religion had been revealed to him. It was based on belief in a single god, Allah, and he called it Islam, meaning "submission to God's will".

Mohammed and his followers, who are called Muslims, spread the new faith throughout Arabia and beyond. Soon it became the basis of a new and growing empire, which brought learning, art and science to peoples as far afield as Morocco and Persia.

The early Muslims sent out missionaries to convert people. They were followed by Arab merchants, who traversed the desert with processions of camels, known as caravans, trading in luxuries such as precious stones, metals and incense.

◀ DOME OF THE ROCK
The Dome of the Rock in Jerusalem is the oldest surviving mosque, or place of Muslim worship. It was built at a place where Mohammed was said to have stopped on his journey to heaven.

Next followed armies, led by the caliph, ruler of the Islamic world. Within 30 years of Mohammed's death, they had conquered a huge area, stretching from Tunisia in the west to Persia in the east. Later, Islamic armies pushed even farther afield, conquering Spain and reaching the borders of India.

Islam was based on the Qur'an, the Muslim sacred book. Muslims were expected to learn how to read Arabic so that they could read the Qur'an. This meant that the Islamic empire became highly educated. Schools were attached to every mosque and universities were founded in major cities such as Baghdad. Muslim scholars also collected information from all the conquered countries. Soon the Islamic

SCHOLARSHIP
Baghdad was a focus of culture and learning and Muslim scientists were famous worldwide. Arab scholars studied the stars, mathematics, medicine, engineering, history, geography and philosophy. Islam tolerated other religions so Christian and Jewish scholars were also welcome.

▲ ASTROLABE
Islamic scientists developed the astrolabe. A flat disc with a rod that could be pointed to the sun or stars, it helped Arab sailors find their way.

◀ CALLIGRAPHY
The art of calligraphy, or beautiful handwriting, was one of the many arts that flourished in the Islamic world.

▼ HOUSE OF LEARNING
Islamic scholars study in a mosque, a Muslim place of worship. Arabic textbooks, particularly in medicine, were used in Europe for centuries.

▲ BAGHDAD
Through the centuries, Baghdad has survived repeated damage by wars, floods and fire. Today it is home to millions of Muslims.

▶ SPREADING ISLAM
Arabian merchants blazed new trails across the deserts to spread the new faith. They crossed western Asia and northern Africa.

empire contained the world's finest scientists, doctors and most able writers. The arts also flourished and houses and mosques were decorated with beautiful tiles and stonework.

Religious faith, learning and a powerful army made the Islamic empire successful and long lasting. It survived until the 13th century.

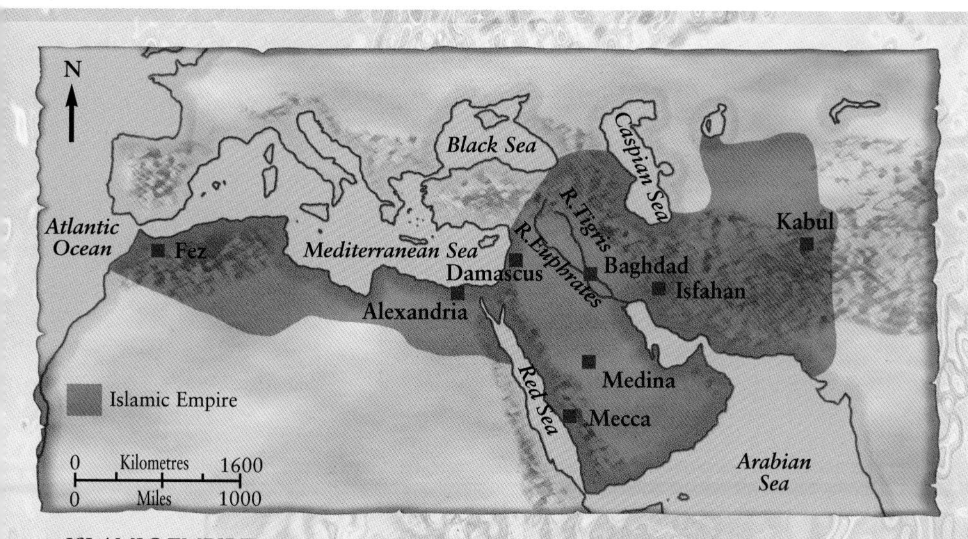

▲ ISLAMIC EMPIRE
The Islamic empire reached its height in AD750, as shown in the map. In some areas, such as Spain, Muslim rule lasted for hundreds of years. In other areas, such as North Africa and much of western Asia, large Muslim communities continue to exist to this day and Muslims can now be found all over the world.

Key Dates

- AD632 Death of Mohammed.
- AD634 The first caliph, Abu Bakr, conquers Arabia.
- AD635–642 Muslims conquer Syria, Egypt, and Persia.
- AD661 The beginning of the Omayyad dynasty.
- AD698 Muslim soldiers capture Carthage.
- AD711 Muslims begin to invade Spain. The empire expands to include northeastern India.
- AD750 Abbasid dynasty founded.
- AD762 Baghdad becomes the Abbasid capital.

Indus Valley Civilization

In around 2500BC, a mysterious civilization grew up on the plain of the Indus River, in what is now Pakistan. Archaeologists have so far been unable to read their writing, find out what their religion was, or work out why their civilization collapsed. But we do know that the Indus Valley people were very successful. They farmed the fertile soil by the Indus and used clay from the river banks to make bricks. With these they built several huge cities.

Most of what we know about the Indus Valley Civilization comes from the remains of their great cities Mohenjo-Daro and Harappa. They built them on the flood plain of the river. Because the river flooded regularly, they constructed massive mud-brick platforms to raise the buildings above the level of the flood waters.

▲ GODDESS
Small clay figures showing a woman with a decorative head-dress, have been found at Mohenjo-Daro. These were most likely representations of a fertility or mother-goddess.

Each city was divided into two areas. One was where the people lived. Flat-roofed, mud-brick houses were arranged in neat rows along straight streets and alleyways. Most houses had a courtyard, a well for water, and even built-in toilets with drains to take the waste to sewers beneath the streets.

The other half of each city was a walled area containing the larger buildings – a public bath, a great hall, and a massive granary, or grain store, the size of an Olympic swimming pool. Priests and worshippers may have used the baths for ritual washing before religious ceremonies. Near the granaries were large threshing floors where farmers brought their grain to be threshed before selling it to the people of the city.

The Indus civilization continued for about 800 years but then began to decline. Houses fell into ruin and many people left. No one knows for certain why this happened. Bad floods and a rising population may have forced farmers to grow too much food, exhausting the land and causing poor harvests and famine.

◀ GOD-KING
A stone bust showing a man dressed in a patterned shawl. The quality of the carving and the thoughtful expression may mean that the man was an Indus god or perhaps a king.

DAILY LIFE

From the evidence, it seems that Indus Valley cities were full of life and activity. Archaeologists have found weights and measuring sticks, which suggests that they were trading areas. Merchants and traders probably thronged the streets, which also contained skilled craftworkers. Farmers too brought their crops into the cities to sell.

▲ GAME PLAYING
Archaeologists have found board games and toy animals showing that Indus people enjoyed playing games.

◀ CLAY SEALS
Stone seals, such as this, probably belonged to merchants who used them to "sign" documents and property. Seals featured an animal, such as bull, antelope, water buffalo, or tiger, each of which was found in the region.

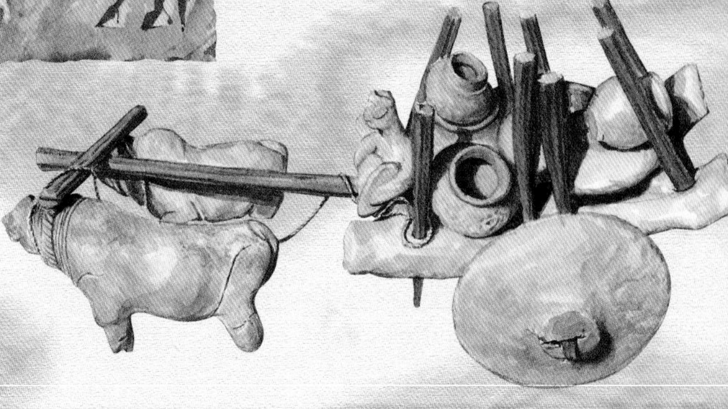

▶ CART MODEL
Small clay models, such as this one, pulled by a pair of bullocks, prove that the Indus people used the wheel. They would have used full-size carts to carry grain and other produce.

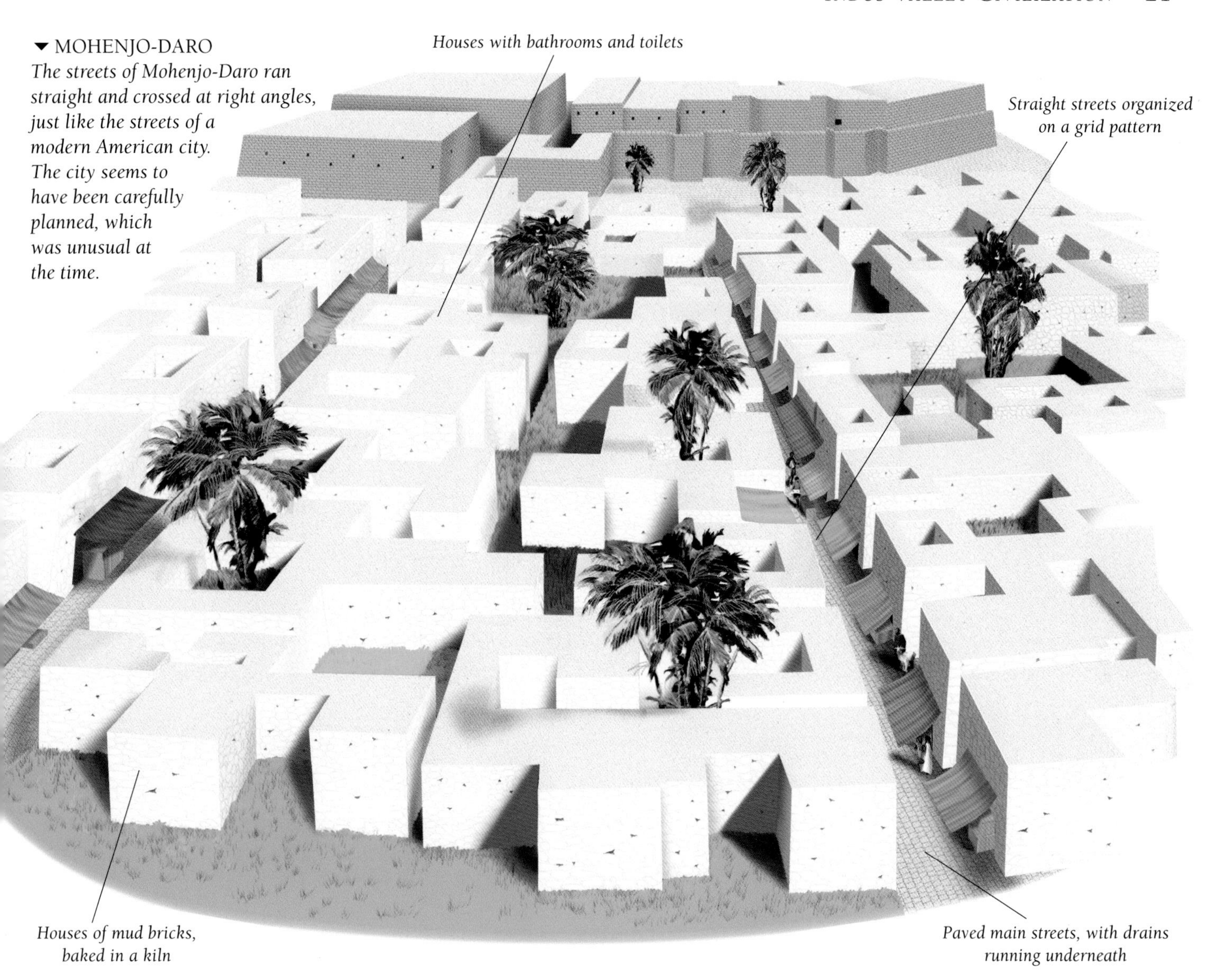

▼ MOHENJO-DARO
The streets of Mohenjo-Daro ran straight and crossed at right angles, just like the streets of a modern American city. The city seems to have been carefully planned, which was unusual at the time.

▶ INDUS VALLEY
The map shows the extent of the Indus Valley Civilization. It was based around its great cities, such as Mohenjo-Daro and Harappa, but many people lived in the country in small towns and villages, making their living on the land. They became rich growing corn to trade in the cities, adding to their diet by hunting wild animals. They were also probably the first people to grow cotton as fabric for clothes.

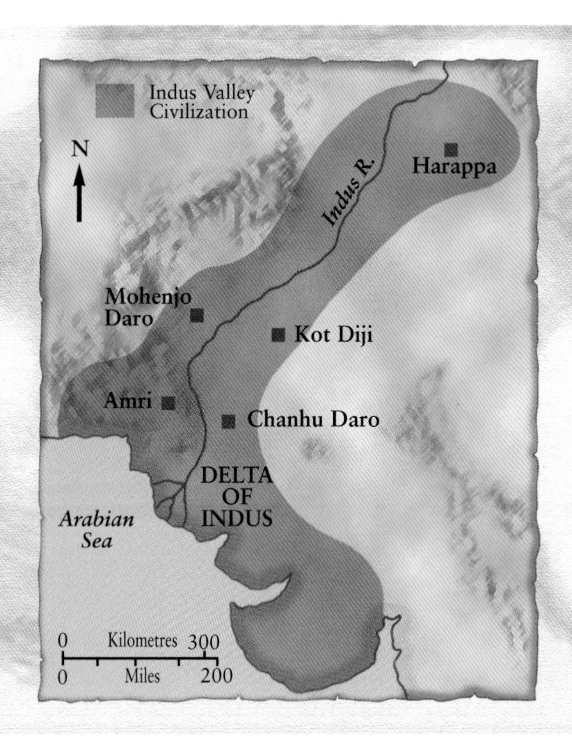

Key Dates

- 3500BC Groups of farmers settle in scattered communities in the Indus Valley.
- 2500BC First Indus cities built.
- 1800BC Decline of Indus Cities begins. Population falls and cities are poorly maintained.
- 1000BC Much of population has shifted to Ganges Valley.
- c.1500BC Aryan peoples from the northwest invade Indus Valley. Invasions may have been a cause of cities' destruction.

Mauryan India

▲ BATTLE OF KALINGA
A noble Indian warrior. In 261BC, Asoka conquered the kingdom of Kalinga. Hundreds of thousands of people were killed. The cruelty of the battle changed Asoka for ever.

MORE THAN ONE thousand years after the decline of the Indus Valley Civilization, a new and glorious empire emerged in the Indian subcontinent. It was known as the Mauryan empire, after the Mauryan dynasty, or ruling family. Between 322BC and 185BC, the Mauryan emperors brought peace and Buddhism into war-torn India and united that vast area for the first time.

India's huge subcontinent has always been home to a huge variety of peoples with different languages, beliefs and customs. By the 6th century BC, there were 16 separate states in northern India alone. Most were based around mud-brick cities along the Ganges River. The Ganges cities were often at war with each other, competing for fertile land. In the 4th century BC, one kingdom in the northwest, Magadha, emerged as a major power and began to defeat nearby settlements. Its leader was Chandragupta Maurya, a nobleman and warrior.

Chandragupta drove out Greek invaders and built an empire that included the whole of northern India from the Hindu Kush to Bengal. His son continued the expansion but it was under his grandson, Asoka, that the Mauryan empire reached its greatest glory.

Asoka began with further conquests, including the kingdom of Kalinga, but he was shocked by the destruction of war. He decided to become a Buddhist and determined that others should follow his new faith of peace and non-violence.

Asoka sent out missionaries and ordered messages about his beliefs to be put up all over his empire. Buddhist texts and sayings were carved on pillars and specially smoothed cliff faces. They explained his belief that everyone is responsible for the welfare of others. They also instructed people to tolerate the beliefs of others and always to avoid violence.

Inspired by his new faith, Asoka built hospitals and introduced new laws. A network of roads was built that connected towns throughout the empire. Farming improved and trade expanded. The Mauryan empire brought peace and prosperity to many parts of India. However, it needed Asoka's leadership to hold it together. After his death, the empire fell apart when Brihadnatha, the last Mauryan emperor, was killed.

RELIGION
Two of the world's great religions – Hinduism and Buddhism – came from India. Hinduism dates back some 4,000 years. Asoka introduced Buddhism. By the end of the Mauryan period it was the most widespread faith in northern India. Asoka also sent Buddhist teachers to nearby countries, such as Burma, to spread the faith.

◀ COLUMN
Asoka's columns were usually topped with one or more lions. Sayings on the column written in local script told people to avoid violence, eat vegetarian food and respect the beliefs of others. They also reminded everyone of how Asoka's rule helped ordinary people, by building roads, rest houses and wells.

◀ BUDDHA
The founder of Buddhism was Siddhartha Gautama, an Indian prince who was born in 563BC.

▲ RAMAYANA
An Indian miniature shows a scene from one of India's great epic poems, the *Ramayana*. Its hero, Rama, was identified with the Hindu god, Vishnu.

◀ HOLY RIVER
Indians have bathed in the River Ganges for centuries although the temples may not have been there during the time of the Mauryans. To Hindus, the Ganges is sacred. It is believed that bathing in its waters washes away sins.

▲ STUPA
The Mauryans built Buddhist shrines, called stupas, in the form of dome-shaped massive mounds, sometimes known as "temple mountains". Asoka built many stupas. One of the oldest to survive is at Sanchi, in central India.

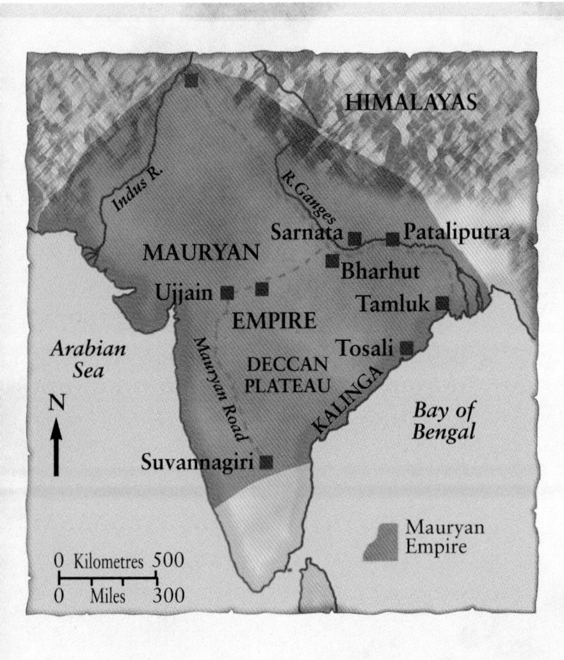

◀ MAURYAN EMPIRE
The map shows the Mauryan Empire at the time of Asoka. His grandfather, Chandragupta, took control of much of northern India, and also made conquests in Pakistan and Afghanistan. Chandragupta's son, Bindusara, conquered large areas of central and southern India, although the southern tip remained unconquered.

Key Dates

- 327–325BC The Macedonian leader, Alexander the Great, conquers the Indus Valley and the Punjab.
- 322BC Chandragupta Maurya takes over the Punjab and founds Mauryan empire.
- 303BC Chandragupta conquers the Indus Valley and part of Afghanistan.
- 301BC Bindusara, Chandragupta's son, comes to the throne and extends the Mauryan empire.
- 269–232BC Reign of Asoka. Buddhism becomes state religion and Mauryan empire flourishes.
- 184BC The death of Brihadnatha, the last Mauryan emperor.

Ancient Egypt

▲ THE NARMER PALETTE *The slate shows Narmer. He was also called Menes, meaning "the founder".*

FIVE THOUSAND YEARS AGO, a great civilization – that of Egypt – emerged in northern Africa. Ruled by all-powerful pharaohs, ancient Egypt dominated the region for three thousand years and was one of the most successful of the ancient civilizations.

The Egyptian civilization began with Narmer. In about 3100BC, he unified two kingdoms – Upper and Lower Egypt – and became the first king or pharaoh. The pharaoh was the most powerful and important person in the kingdom and was believed to have the same status as a god. Under Narmer, and the pharaohs who followed, Egypt prospered. To help them wield their power, the pharaohs trained a civil service of scribes or writers. The scribes recorded and collected taxes and carried out the day-to-day running of the kingdom, which was divided into a number of districts. Merchants journeyed to nearby areas such as Palestine, Syria and Nubia, and the Egyptian army followed, occupying some of these areas for a while.

The land of ancient Egypt was dry and inhospitable and the Egyptians relied on the great River Nile for survival. It was the life blood of the region and provided everything – fertilizer for the land, water for farming and irrigation, and a highway for Egyptian boats, called "feluccas", which were some of the world's earliest sailing craft.

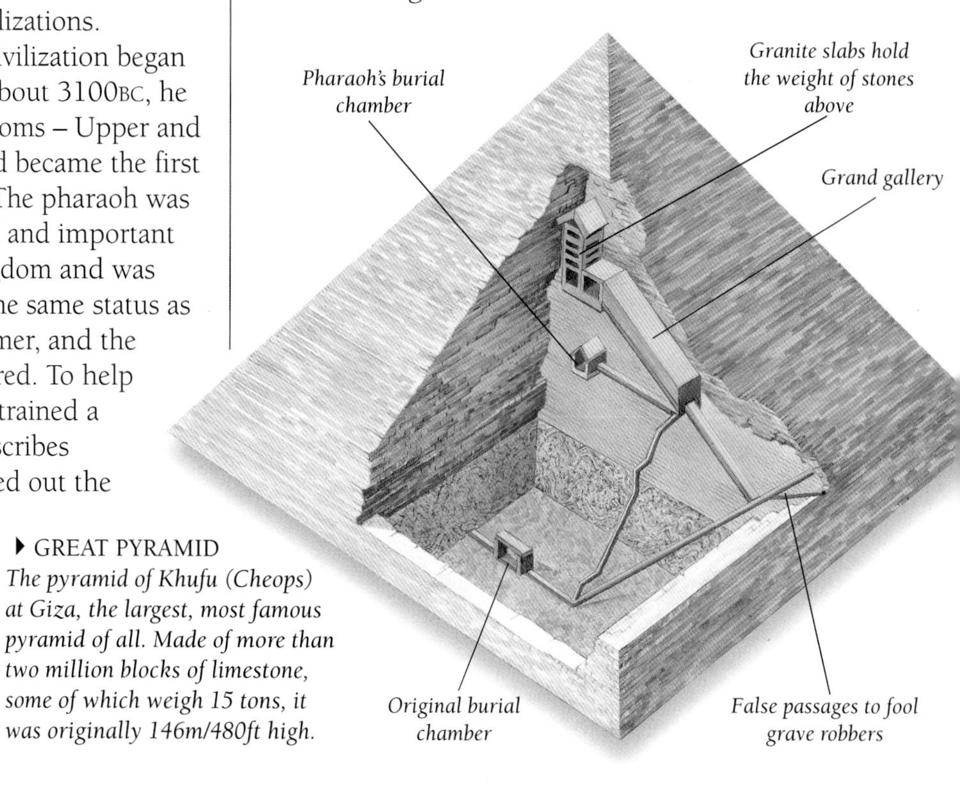

▶ GREAT PYRAMID *The pyramid of Khufu (Cheops) at Giza, the largest, most famous pyramid of all. Made of more than two million blocks of limestone, some of which weigh 15 tons, it was originally 146m/480ft high.*

AFTERLIFE

The Egyptians believed in life after death. They also believed that their pharaohs were gods, who would continue living after their bodies had died. For this reason they built the pyramids to safeguard their bodies.

▶ THE SPHINX Half pharaoh, half lion, the great Sphinx at Giza symbolized royal power. Some 18m/60ft high and 55m/180ft long, it was carved out of limestone rock in about 2620BC.

▲ THE GREAT PYRAMIDS The pyramid of Chephren, pictured above, dates from 2560BC. The top of the original flat casing still survives. Many pyramids had steps on the outside. Tens of thousands of workers were needed to build the great pyramids.

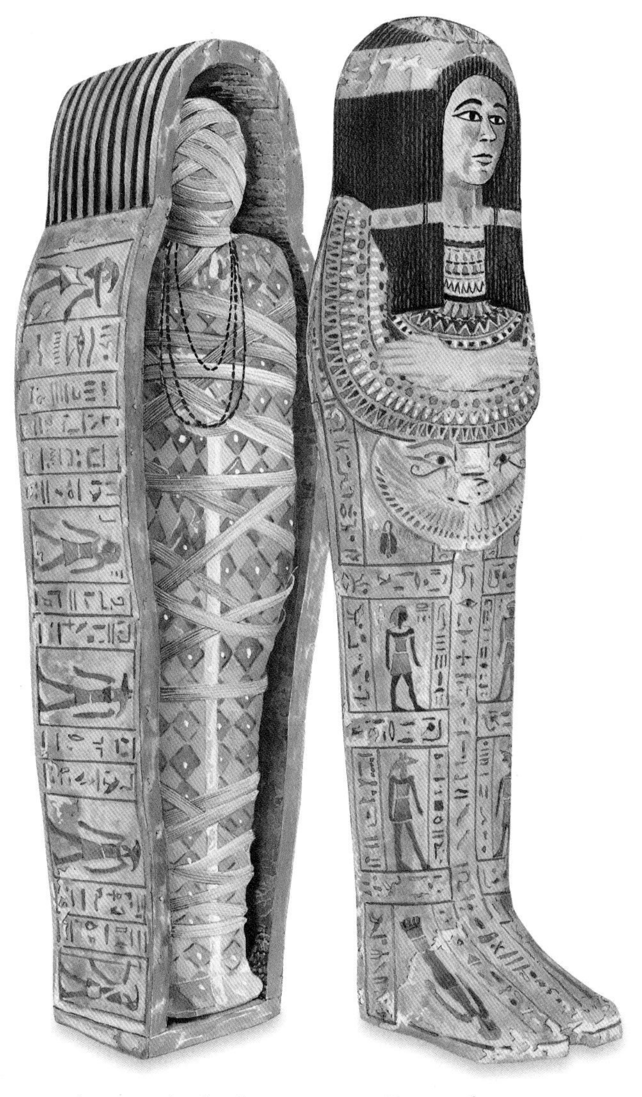

Body wrapped in bandages

Decorated mummy case

Once a year the Nile flooded, its rich silt nourishing the land on either side. All the land watered by the river was needed for cultivation, but during the floods, no one could work the land. This was when all the able-bodied men of the kingdom went to work on large-scale building projects, such as cities and temples to the many gods of Egypt. They also built the great pyramids, the tombs and last resting places of the pharaohs and some of the biggest stone structures ever built. The desert lands were where these burial tombs were built.

◀ MUMMIFICATION
When a pharaoh died, his body was preserved. The inner organs were removed and the body was treated with a chemical and then wrapped in linen bandages. The "mummy" was then put in a decorated coffin and left in the pyramid tomb.

▶ CLOTHING
Egyptian clothes were usually made of linen, woven from flax. The richer the person, the more fine the cloth.

◀ BRICK MAKING
Tomb paintings tell us much about Egyptian daily life. Here Egyptian craftspeople make building bricks using soft clay from the Nile, combined with straw.

▲ HIEROGLYPHICS
The Egyptians invented a form of picture writing, now known as hieroglyphics. There were more than 700 different picture signs, each one corresponding to one sound or word.

▼ PAPYRUS
The Egyptians invented a kind of paper, called papyrus. They made it from the stems of papyrus reeds that grew beside the Nile. The English word "paper" comes from the word papyrus.

Ancient Egypt

▲ RAMESES II
This huge statue of Rameses II, who reigned from 1304 to 1237BC, stands in front of the great temple of Abu Simbel. It was one of many monuments that he had built to remind Egyptians of his power.

PHARAOHS RULED ancient Egypt for the whole of its long 3,000-year history. The later pharaohs, from the period known as the New Kingdom, were the most powerful. They extended the empire, and sent ambassadors all over western Asia. They built huge temples and erected colossal statues of themselves. For about 500 years, New Kingdom Egypt was the world's most magnificent civilization.

The Egyptians believed their pharaohs were gods. To them the pharaoh was both Horus, the falcon-headed sky god, and Amun-Re, the sun god. This god-like status gave the pharaohs absolute power. They appointed the priests, as well as all civil servants and chief ministers. They also controlled the army, which grew large with recruits from conquered regions all the way from Sudan to Syria.

Everywhere they went ordinary Egyptians were reminded of the pharaoh's power. In front of the temples were massive stone statues of the king in the guise of the sun god. Carved inscriptions told anyone who could read of the pharaoh's godly rank. People also read of the pharaohs' victories in Palestine and Nubia and of their peace treaties with the Hittites of Turkey.

▶ TUTANKHAMUN
Pharaoh Tutankhamun was only 18 when he died. However, he is the most famous pharaoh because when archaeologists found his tomb in the 1920s, its contents, including his golden death mask, were still complete.

◀ TOMB TREASURES
Most ancient Egyptian tombs were robbed hundreds of years ago, but when Tutankhamun's tomb was opened up, it still contained everything that had been buried with him, including food, furniture, jewels and his glittering gold coffin.

EGYPTIAN WOMEN
Women of all classes in ancient Egypt had many rights, compared to women later in history. They ran the household and controlled their own property. They followed skilled professions; such as midwifery, served as priestesses, and could hold important positions at court.

◀ NEFERTITI
The wife of the New Kingdom pharaoh Akhenaten was Queen Nefertiti. She ruled with her husband, assisted in religious ceremonies, and had a strong political influence.

▲ HUNTING
Egyptians enjoyed hunting. The pharaoh and nobles hunted in the desert, where they caught antelopes, gazelles and wild oxen. They also hunted geese and other waterfowl on the banks of the Nile.

◀ TOMB WORKERS
The workers who built the royal tombs lived in Deir el-Medineh, a village specially built for them in the desert. When they died they were buried in tombs in the cliffs above the village. At work, they were divided into gangs of 60 craftsmen for each tomb. They were supervised by a foreman and worked an eight-hour day, eight or nine days at a stretch but they were well rewarded. Once, they went on strike when rations failed to arrive. It may have been the first recorded strike.

The most famous of the Egyptian pharaohs came from the New Kingdom. They included Rameses II and Seti I, who were renowned military leaders, Akhenaten, who briefly abolished all the gods except for the sun god, the boy-king Tutankhamun, and Hatshepsut, a powerful queen who ruled with all the might of her male relatives.

After the glory of the New Kingdom, Egypt survived numerous invasions and changes of pharaoh. The last ruler of an independent ancient Egypt was Queen Cleopatra VII, famous for her love for the Roman leader Mark Antony. Much Egyptian culture, from its gods to its funeral customs, survived, but after Cleopatra's death in 30BC, Egypt became part of the huge Roman empire.

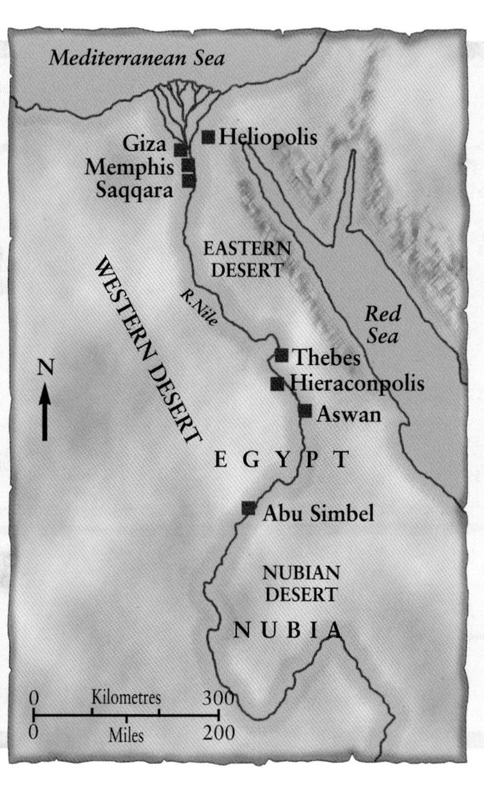

◀ ANCIENT EGYPT
The map shows the extent of ancient Egypt. Lower Egypt was in the north. The kingdom of Upper Egypt was in the south. Farther south still was Nubia, a source of precious materials such as gold and ivory, which the Egyptians later conquered.

Key Dates

- 3100–2686BC Upper and Lower Egypt are united.
- 2686–2181BC Old Kingdom. The pharaohs build up their power and are buried in pyramids.
- 2182–2040BC The pharaohs' power breaks down and two rulers govern Egypt from separate capital cities, Heracleopolis and Thebes.
- 2040–1786BC Middle Kingdom.
- 1786–1567BC Invasion forces sent to Egypt from Syria and Palestine.
- 1570–1085BC New Kingdom. Egyptian pharaohs rule once more and the civilization flourishes.
- 1083–333BC The empire collapses. Egypt divides into separate states.
- 333–323BC Egypt becomes part of Alexander the Great's empire.

African Civilizations

AFRICA IS A HUGE and ancient continent. Its northern region produced the great Egyptian civilization. But further south, below the Sahara desert that divides the continent, other civilizations and kingdoms also appeared. Many were skilled metalworking cultures that produced tools, beautiful adornments and fine sculptures. They sent merchants on long trading journeys. Some merchants crossed the vast Sahara desert with their camels, braving heat and drought to reach the ports of the Red Sea coast and the trading posts of North Africa.

African civilizations were scattered far and wide across the continent. But there were several main areas. Ghana, Benin, Mali and Songhai were small kingdoms that flourished, at different times, in West Africa. The people were Bantu speakers, descendants of the Bantus, farmers and herders who originated in West Africa about 4,000 years ago. They opened up trade links with the Muslim rulers of North Africa, sending ivory, ebony, gold, copper and slaves northwards and bringing back manufactured goods such as pottery and glassware. They learned how to work iron, perhaps from people in North African cities such as Carthage. As demand for their goods increased, their kingdoms flourished.

There were also numerous trading kingdoms in East Africa. The most famous was on the Zimbabwe plateau. Here the Shona people had fertile land and rich sources of copper and gold. Their merchants reached the east coast of Africa, where they traded with ships coming from

▲ BENIN BRONZES
Craft workers from Benin, in what is now Nigeria, made beautiful cast bronze figures – such as this head of a royal woman.

▶ AXUM
The Ethiopian kingdom of Axum traded with India and the Islamic world. Its rulers built a palace at Takaji Mariam and many stone obelisks, some up to 30m/100ft high. Most people lived in small thatched huts.

EARLIEST CIVILIZATIONS
South of Egypt, the first civilization to emerge in Africa was the kingdom of Kush, which flourished on the Nile from about 500BC to AD350. Its capital was Meroe, an important iron-working area. From about 500BC, metal working spread south to other parts of Africa.

◀ GOLD
Skilled gold workers from the ancient kingdom of Kush made this gold papyrus holder in about 590BC. Much later, African gold workers, especially from Ghana and Mali, became famous all over the world.

▲ ROCK PAINTINGS
Sub-Saharan Africa is rich in rock paintings. This one was painted in the West African kingdom of Mali, which flourished between AD1200–1500.

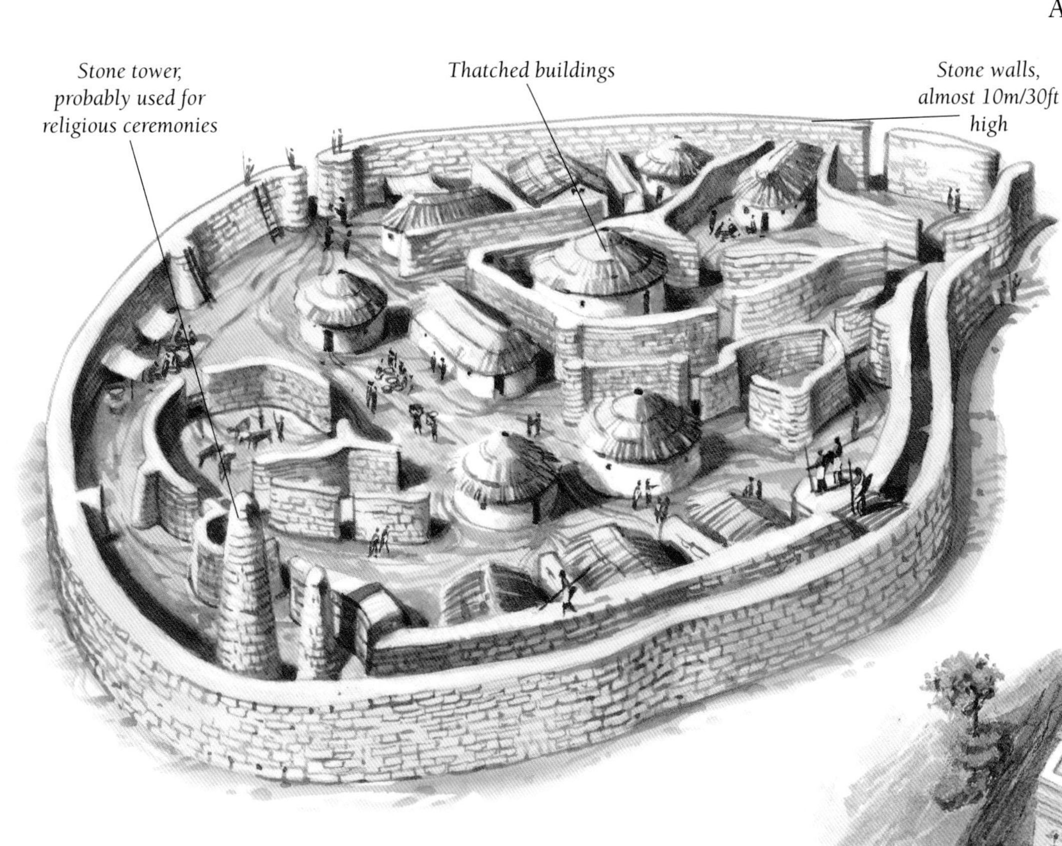

◀ GREAT ZIMBABWE
The great oval stone enclosure at Great Zimbabwe was the heart of the Shona empire. Its stone walls still stand today and contain the remains of several buildings, possibly the ruler's home.

▼ LALIBELA
Some areas of Africa converted to Islam but Axum became Christian in the 4th century. By the 1200s, local masons had carved entire churches, such as this one, from rocky outcrops at Lalibela, southeast of Axum.

India, the Islamic empire and even China. Further north were still more trading and metalworking kingdoms in what are now Zambia and Ethiopia.

The people of the African kingdoms led lives that were well adapted to their environment. They sought out good land for crops and cattle, and found good sources of metal ore. Their kingdoms lasted a long time and many remained prosperous until the Europeans colonized Africa in the 19th century.

▶ AFRICAN CIVILIZATIONS
The peoples of Africa settled along fertile river valleys and in areas where there were sources of metals such as iron and gold. Soon even the inhospitable Sahara Desert had its settlements, oases and stopping-places for merchants. The Sahara also provided salt, one of the most valuable substances in the ancient world.

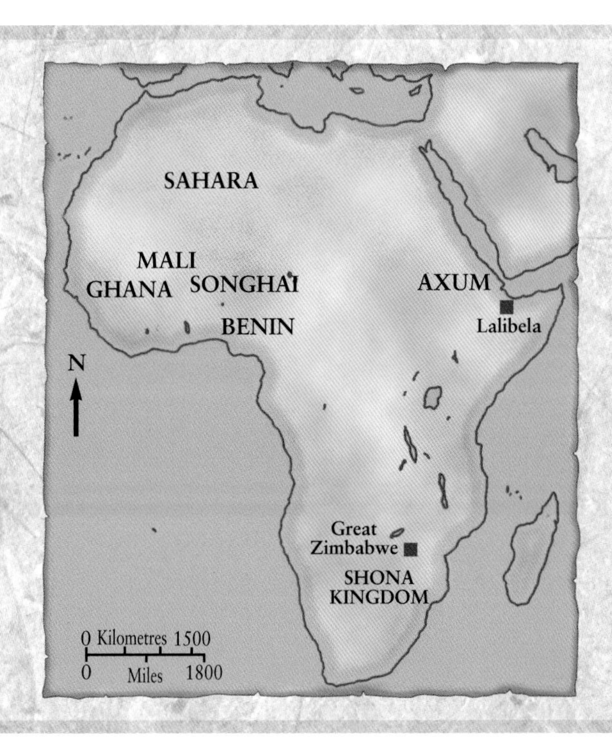

Key Dates

- AD320–650 Kingdom of Axum, East Africa.
- AD700–1200 Kingdom of Ghana, West Africa.
- AD1100–1897 Kingdom of Benin, West Africa.
- AD1200–1500 Kingdom of Mali, West Africa.
- AD1270–1450 Great Zimbabwe is capital of Shona kingdom.
- AD1350–600 Kingdom of Songhai, West Africa.

Minoan Crete

▲ FISHERMAN
A young Minoan fisherman holds fish caught from the Mediterranean Sea. The Minoans were seafarers. Fishing was the basis of their economy.

JUST OVER 100 YEARS AGO, British archaeologist Arthur Evans made an extraordinary discovery. He unearthed the ruins of an ancient and beautifully decorated palace at Knossos, on the Mediterranean island of Crete. The palace was enormous. It had hundreds of rooms, courtyards and winding staircases. It reminded Evans of the ancient Greek story of the labyrinth, a maze-like structure built by the legendary Cretan king Minos. He did not know who had built the palace, so he called its builders Minoans, after the mythical king.

Remains in the palace gave many clues so today we know much more about the Minoans. They may originally have come from mainland Greece. They migrated to Crete where, for nearly 1,000 years, they created a rich and wonderful culture that reached its height between 2000 and 1700BC. Seas teeming with fish and a rich fertile soil meant that the Minoans had a prosperous and comfortable lifestyle.

The Minoans built many palaces on Crete but Knossos was the largest. The building contained shrines, religious symbols and statues of goddesses. There were several large and lavishly decorated rooms, probably royal throne rooms. Some smaller rooms were full of tall jars, called pithoi, which would have held oil, wine and other produce. Possibly a priest-ruler lived at Knossos, which may also have been an important area for food and trade.

Walls in the Cretan palaces were covered in beautiful paintings, many of which have survived. Some show natural scenes and others show the Minoan people working, enjoying themselves and taking part in religious ceremonies.

◀ WALL PAINTING
The palace at Knossos contained about 1300 rooms. Many were decorated with wall paintings like this one showing a beautiful Minoan woman with long braided hair.

◀ SNAKE GODDESS
A pottery goddess from Knossos wears typical Minoan clothing – an open bodice and pleated skirt. Her snakes may symbolize fertility.

BULLS AND MINOTAURS
According to Greek myth, Crete was ruled by King Minos. He was the son of Europa, granddaughter of the sea god Poseidon and Zeus, ruler of the gods. Poseidon sent Minos a magnificent white bull for sacrifice. Bulls were sacred to the Minoans and their images appear throughout Knossos.

◀ SLAYING THE MINOTAUR
Theseus, the Greek hero, slays the Minotaur, a monster who was half man, half bull. According to Greek myth, Minos kept the Minotaur in a labyrinth or maze. Every year, young men and women were sacrificed to him.

▲ BULL LEAPING
A wall painting shows young Minoan men and women leaping over the backs of bulls. This daring feat was probably part of a religious ceremony that took place in the courtyard at Knossos.

▼ STORAGE JAR
Hundreds of these earthenware storage jars, or pithoi, have been found at Knossos, many as tall as a grown man.

◀ DAILY LIFE
Minoan towns were full of bustle and life. Most were near the coast. Houses were brightly painted and usually two or three levels high. Olive trees grew on the island and olives were used for oil and cooking.

The Minoans were seafarers. They traded with many countries, importing copper from Turkey, ivory and gold from Egypt and lapis lazuli from Afghanistan.

Suddenly, this flourishing culture suffered a disaster. Palace walls collapsed and there were great fires. Possibly this was due to a massive earthquake or a volcanic eruption on the nearby island of Thera. The Minoans rebuilt their palaces but in 1450BC disaster struck again. Myceneans invaded from mainland Greece and the Minoan civilization was overrun.

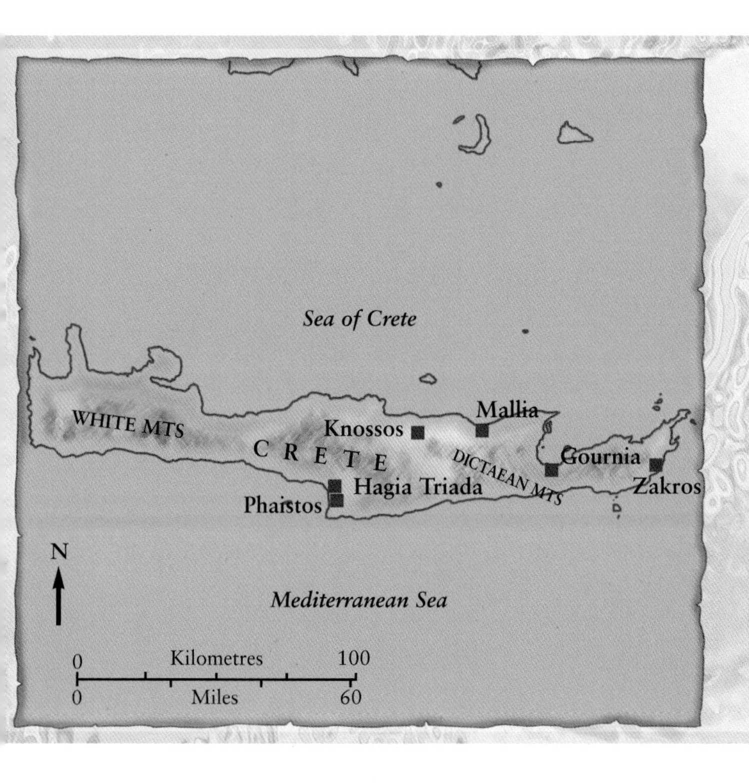

Key Dates

- c.6000BC Mainland Greeks arrive in Crete.
- 2000BC Minoans build palace at Knossos.
- 2000–1700BC Minoans build palaces at Phaistos, Mallia and Zakros. Minoan culture flourishes.
- 1900BC Cretans use potter's wheel.
- 1450BC Minoan civilization collapses with eruption on Thera and the arrival of invaders from Greece.

◀ MINOAN CIVILIZATION
Crete is the largest Greek island and the birthplace of the Minoan culture, one of the first European civilizations. The map shows the extent of this glorious civilization. Apart from the Palace of Minos in Knossos, the Minoans also built fabulous palaces in Mallia, Phaistos and Zakros and established trading posts throughout the Mediterranean.

Mycenae

In about 1600BC a warlike group came to power in mainland Greece. They were the Mycenaeans, called after one of their largest strongholds at Mycenae in the northeastern Peloponnese. The Mycenaeans created the first Greek civilization. They lived in massive hilltop citadels or fortified settlements, made stunning gold objects and produced soldiers who were famed for their bravery.

The Mycenaeans probably consisted of several different groups of people, each with their own ruler. Each group was based in its own citadel. Mycenae was the largest but there were others at Tiryns and Gla. The people all spoke an early form of Greek and their massive fortifications were built with such huge stones that people later thought that giants must have hauled the stones into place.

From their native Greek mainland, the Mycenaeans voyaged far into the Aegean and Mediterranean Seas. Their merchants went west to Sicily and east to the Turkish coast, where they set up a trading post called Miletus. They also visited many of the Greek islands, trading with local people or setting up colonies. Their greatest conquest was the large island of Crete, where they defeated the Minoans. This conquest gave them access to many new trade routes that Minoan merchants had used.

▲ MASK OF "AGAMEMNON"
This beautiful gold mask would have belonged to a Mycenaean king. When the king was buried, the mask was placed over his face. Archaeologists once thought the mask was a portrait of Agamemnon, a hero of the Trojan War.

The ruins left by the Mycenaeans look very bleak today, with their bare stone walls on windswept hillsides. But the kings and nobles did themselves proud, building small but luxurious palaces inside their citadels. Each citadel also contained houses for the king's soldiers, officials, priests, scribes and craftworkers. Farmers settled in the hill country and surrounding plains. They supplied the king and his people with food and sheltered in the citadel during times of war.

The Mycenaean civilization continued until about 1200BC when a great fire destroyed the citadel of Mycenae. Although the Mycenaeans hung on for another 100 years, their power began to decline.

▲ WARRIOR
Mycenaean warriors wore finely decorated helmets and highly elaborate battle dress. They were very important in Mycenaean society.

THE TROJAN WAR
Ancient Greek myths tell of a great war between Greece and Troy. Paris, Prince of Troy, fell in love and ran away with Helen, Queen of Sparta and wife of King Menelaus. King Menelaus, his brother Agamemnon and a huge army beseiged Troy for 10 years, finally capturing the city. Historians believe the legend is based on a real battle involving the Mycenaeans.

▶ THE TROJAN HORSE
The Greeks tricked the Trojans with a huge wooden horse. They pretended to leave Troy, leaving the horse behind. The Trojans pulled the horse into the city. Hidden inside were Greeks. Late at night, they came out of the horse and captured Troy. This modern-day version of the horse was designed by the Turkish architect Izzet Senemoglu and is a popular tourist attraction.

◂ MYCENAE
The Mycenaeans built their huge citadels on the tops of hills, near to the coast. Farmlands stretched back on to the inland plains. Huge walls surrounded the citadels. Some said the walls had been built by Cyclops, the legendary one-eyed giant. Within Mycenae was a palace and many other buildings. A town lay outside the fortification.

▲ SEA CREATURES
The Mycenaeans often decorated objects with sea creatures such as dolphins, or the octopus on this stemmed drinking cup. They valued the sea, which they sailed for trade and conquest.

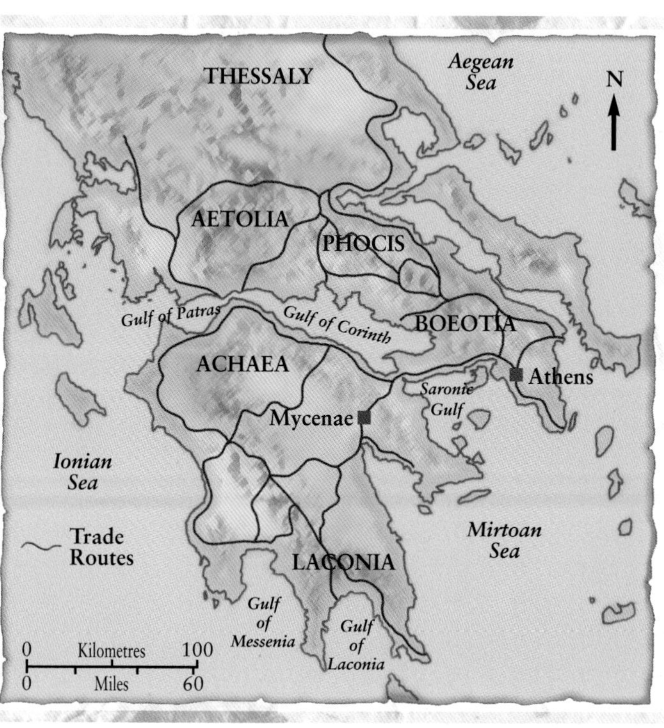

◂ MYCENAEANS
The map shows the main areas of Mycenaean influence and their extensive trading routes. They lived on sites near to the coast. Many of their major citadels were on the Peloponnese, the large peninsula that makes up the southern part of the mainland. There were also major settlements at Athens and around Lake Kopais. From these strongholds, the Mycenaeans sailed to most of the islands in the Aegean Sea.

Key Dates

- 1600BC Mycenaean civilization begins to develop in groups on Greek mainland.
- 1450BC The Mycenaeans invade and conquer the Minoans of Crete.
- 1200BC Decline of Mycenaean civilization.
- 800BC Homer's epic poems, the *Iliad* and the *Odyssey*, record some of the traditions of the Mycenaeans.

The Etruscans

▲ ETRUSCAN POT
Etruscan pottery was often beautifully decorated with abstract designs or pictures of animals. Many skilled craftworkers lived and worked in the cities.

One of the least-known early peoples, the Etruscans lived between the Arno and Tiber rivers in western Italy. From the 8th to the 1st centuries BC, they built a series of cities and grew wealthy by mining copper, tin and iron. We do not know where the Etruscans came from originally, and they remain a mysterious people. They could write, but none of their literature has survived, and many of their cities lie beneath modern Italian towns.

The Etruscans' strength came from living near the coast. They established iron mines by the sea, at Populonia and the nearby island of Elba, and used these as the basis for trade. Skilled seafarers, the Etruscans crossed the Mediterranean to trade with the Phoenician settlers at Carthage, North Africa. They constructed ports for their ships but built their cities slightly inland to safeguard against pirate attacks.

They also traded with Greece but the Greeks began to set up rival trading colonies in southern Italy. By the 6th century BC, the Etruscans and Greeks were at war. The Gauls, ancient people of western Europe, were also making raids. Etruscan leaders realized that their best protection was to join forces, and 12 of their cities came together in a league to encourage trade and defend each other from attack.

The Etruscans were also skilled artists. Their art was stongly influenced by the Greeks. The most spectacular Etruscan remains are tombs. Rich families built large

▲ CHARIOT-RACE MURALS
Etruscans may have been the first people to introduce chariot racing, as shown in this tomb painting from Chiusi. Later, it became a popular Roman pastime.

MUSIC AND DANCE
Archaeologists in the 19th century discovered thousands of Etruscan wall paintings and bronze statues. Many of these show that music and dance were an important part of Etruscan culture.

◀ FLUTE PLAYER
Musical instruments, such as these pipes, may have played a part in religious ceremonies, and in entertainment for the noble families.

▶ LYRE PLAYER
Etruscan musicians probably played the lyre, a sort of small harp, to accompany poetry, songs and dancing.

▲ ROOF DECORATION
This brightly painted head dates from the 6th century BC. Made of clay and fired in a kiln, it decorated the roof of a building in the Etruscan town of Veii.

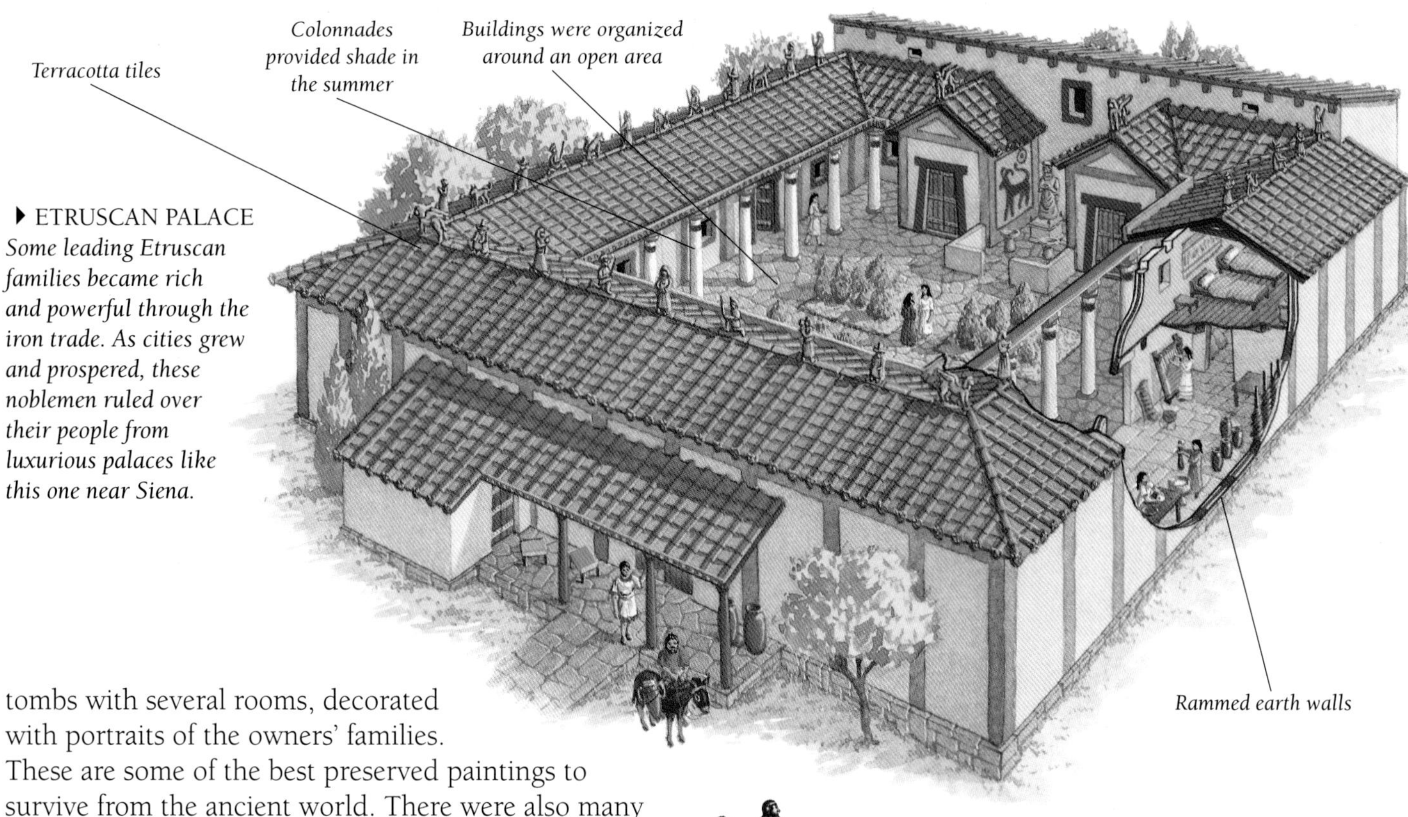

▸ ETRUSCAN PALACE
Some leading Etruscan families became rich and powerful through the iron trade. As cities grew and prospered, these noblemen ruled over their people from luxurious palaces like this one near Siena.

tombs with several rooms, decorated with portraits of the owners' families. These are some of the best preserved paintings to survive from the ancient world. There were also many fine sculptors in the northern Etruscan cities. They worked in bronze, producing figurines, statues, and items such as engraved mirrors and decorative panels for furniture and chariots.

The Romans – the Etruscans' final enemies – prized this artwork highly. When Rome and her allies conquered Etruscan cities in the 3rd century BC, they took away thousands of bronze statues.

◂ TRADE
The Etruscans traded with Phoenicia and Greece, becoming the first wealthy civilization in western Europe. With profits from the iron trade, they could enjoy luxuries such as this gold vase.

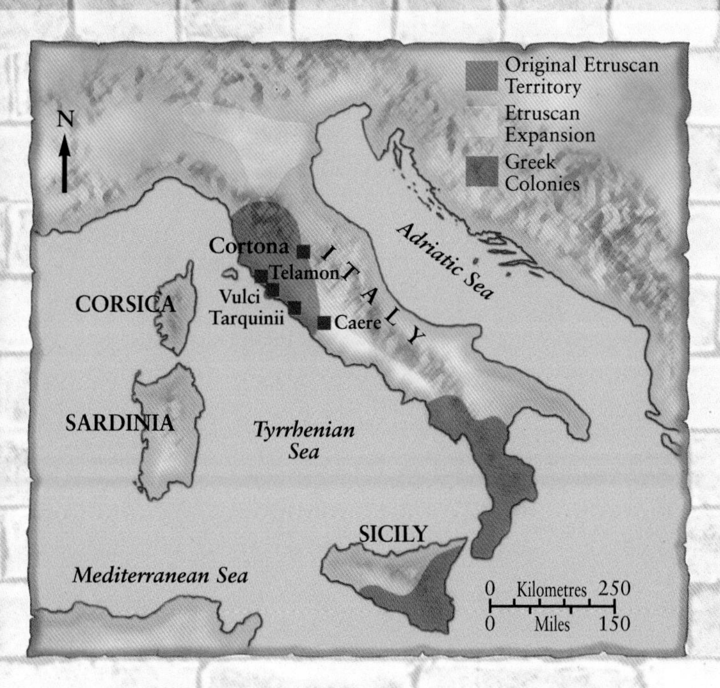

◂ ETRUSCANS
The map shows the extent of Etruscan influence and how this grew. Etruria, the land of the Etruscans, stretched from the River Arno to the Tiber. The major Etruscan cities, such as Caere, Chiusi, and Tarquinia, were independent states with their own rulers. Rome, originally a small town on the edge of Etruria, became a city in the time of the Etruscans.

Key Dates

- 800BC Etruscans set up cities.
- 540BC The Etruscans trade with the Phoenician city of Carthage, and forge an alliance with the Carthaginians.
- 524 and 474BC The Etruscans and Greeks battle over trade in Italy. The Greeks, with colonies in southern Italy, are victorious.
- 413BC The Etruscan league of cities makes an alliance with the Greeks.
- 273BC Romans conquer Caere.
- 265BC Romans destroy Volsinii.

Classical Greece

▲ ZEUS
The Greeks worshipped many gods and goddesses. Zeus, above, was supreme. Greeks thought the gods lived on Mount Olympus, Greece's highest mountain.

THE WAY OUR countries are governed, the books we read, the plays we watch, even many of our sports, all have their origins in the classical Greek civilization, which flourished some 2,500 years ago. The Greeks did not have a huge empire. For much of their history their civilization consisted of several separate city-states. But their art, science, philosophy and ways of life have had an enormous influence on our lives.

The Greek countryside is rocky and mountainous. Early Greeks lived near the coast or in fertile plains between the mountains. Gradually, these early settlements became city-states. The Greeks were good sailors and boat-builders and their civilization began to flourish when they sailed to Italy and the eastern Mediterranean to trade with nearby settlements. They also set up colonies in these areas and around the coast of the Aegean Sea.

As their wealth increased the Greeks built fine cities. The largest and richest was Athens. The citizens of Athens enjoyed much leisure time and Athens became the hub of Greek culture. Greek dramatists such as Sophocles wrote some of the finest plays in western theatre. Their musicians created fine music and architects designed elegant buildings and temples. The Greeks also started the Olympic Games.

◀ PARTHENON
The largest temple on the Acropolis, the Parthenon was built in 432BC. The pillars were marble and its beautiful frieze showed a procession in celebration of the goddess Athene.

Greek education was famous throughout the ancient world. Philosophers, or thinkers, came to Athens to discuss everything from the nature of love to how a country should be governed. The Athenians developed a new form of government, in which people had a say in who ruled them. They called it democracy, or government by the people. Not everyone was actually allowed to vote but their system was the ancestor of modern democratic government.

Athens remained strong for several centuries until the Romans began to take over the Mediterranean world. War with another Greek city state, Sparta, also weakened Athens. In 404BC Sparta defeated Athens.

ENTERTAINMENT
The ancient Greeks believed in enjoying themselves. They enjoyed music and art and went to theatre regularly. Sport too was very important and had religious significance. The first ever Olympic Games were held in 776BC, in tribute to the god Zeus. Like today, they were held every four years.

◀ ATHLETE
A Greek discus thrower. The Olympic Games were only for men. Women were not even allowed to watch. They held their own games, in tribute to Hera, goddess of women.

Actors wore these masks – the one on the left for comedy, that on the right for tragedy.

▲ AMPHITHEATRE
Greek theatres were large, open-air arenas with rows of stone seats. There were regular drama festivals where playwrights such as Aristophanes, Euripides and Sophocles competed for the award of best play.

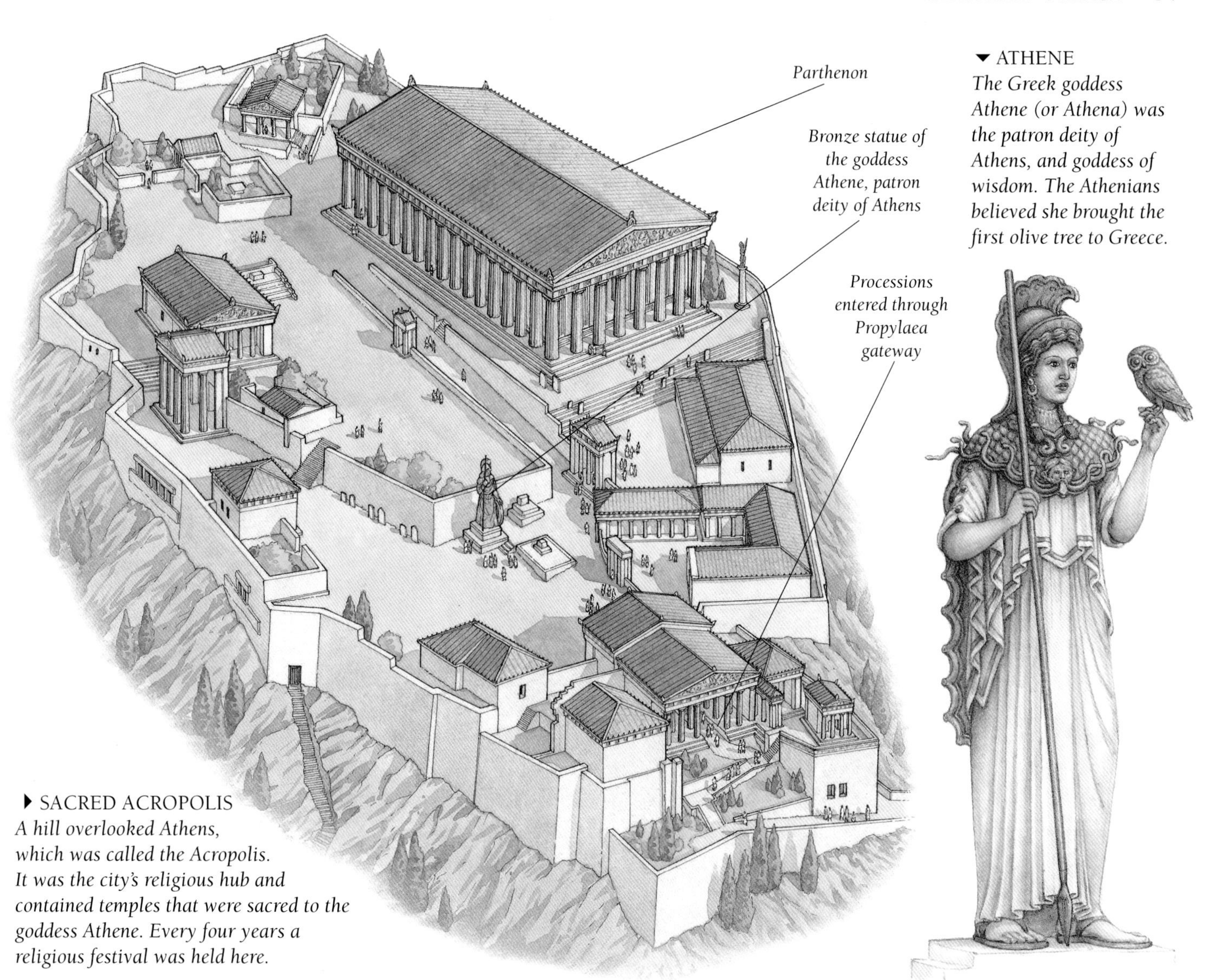

▼ ATHENE
The Greek goddess Athene (or Athena) was the patron deity of Athens, and goddess of wisdom. The Athenians believed she brought the first olive tree to Greece.

▶ SACRED ACROPOLIS
A hill overlooked Athens, which was called the Acropolis. It was the city's religious hub and contained temples that were sacred to the goddess Athene. Every four years a religious festival was held here.

◀ ANCIENT GREECE
The Greeks spread out from their homeland in the Peloponnese, setting up colonies in southern Italy, Sicily, the Aegean, and the coasts of the Black Sea.

▼ ELGIN MARBLES
These marble sculptures, known as the Elgin Marbles, were taken from the Parthenon to England in 1815 by Lord Elgin. They remain in the British Museum.

Classical Greece

The heart of a Greek city was the agora, or market place. This was a central square surrounded by the city's main public buildings – temples, law courts, market halls and shops. Everyone came to the agora to do their shopping, meet friends, listen to scholars, or just gossip. The city council also met in the agora.

Beyond the agora lay streets of private houses. They were usually arranged around a courtyard with overhanging roofs and small windows to keep out the summer sun and winter cold. In the summer, much of the life of the house took place here.

Men and women were not equal in ancient Greece. Women did not have the vote and were allowed little in the way of money or private property. Most women aimed to marry and give birth to a son. Men enjoyed much more freedom. There was even a room in most Greek houses, called the andron, which was used only by the men of the household.

Boys and girls were also treated differently. In the cities, boys went to school from age 7 to 12. They learned reading, writing, music and poetry, as well as sports such as wrestling. Most girls stayed at home with their mothers, where they learned skills such as spinning, weaving and cooking, so that they would be able to run homes of their own.

Life was rather different in Sparta. From early childhood, boys were taught skills to prepare them for fighting and life in the army. All men had to do military service. Girls too were trained for a hard, outdoor life.

When a Greek person died, people believed that he or she would go to Hades, the underworld. The Greeks imagined this as a dark, underground world, surrounded by a river, the Styx. People were buried with a coin, to pay Charon, the ferryman who would row them across the River Styx into the next world.

◀ WOMEN
Greek women wore folded material called chitons, fastened at the shoulder. Few houses had water so, balancing jars on their head, women collected water from the local well or fountain.

◀ VENUS DE MILO
This beautiful statue of Aphrodite is known as the Venus de Milo. Although carved after the time of classical Greece, it still demonstrates the ancient Greek ideal of the perfect body.

LEARNING AND PHILOSOPHY
The Greeks were educated people and valued learning. Western philosophy, which means "love of wisdom" began in ancient Greece. Greek philosophers studied astronomy, science and asked deep questions about the meaning of life.

◀ SOCRATES
The most famous of all the ancient Greek philosophers was Socrates (469–399BC). During discussions, he asked continuous questions, sometimes pretending not to know the answers in an attempt to trip up his opponents.

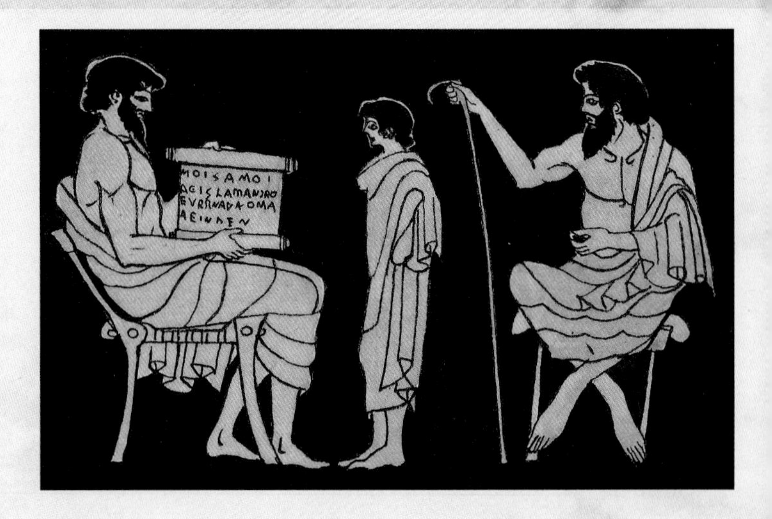

▲ GOING TO SCHOOL
Boys from rich families were taken to school by a slave called a paidogogos. The tutor used papyrus rolls to teach the child, but the boy would learn to write on a wax tablet, using a pointed tool called a stylus.

Courtyard

Clay tiles

Upper floor containing bedrooms

Dining room

Kitchen

▲ GREEK VILLA
Most Greek houses were made of mud bricks, with wooden upper floors and roofs of clay tiles. Most houses had courtyards containing an altar where the householders offered sacrifices to the gods.

▶ SPARTA
Spartan footsoldiers were heavily armed. When attacked, they formed a solid line or phalanx, spears pointing outwards. Sparta was far inland. Its people had to be tough to live in their remote mountain region.

◀ COINS
The Greeks used silver coins. Slaves toiled in mines near Athens, digging out silver by hand. Some coins were decorated with an owl, symbol of the goddess Athene.

Key Dates

- 900BC The Greeks begin to trade in the Mediterranean.
- 776BC First recorded Olympic Games.
- 700BC Greek city states develop.
- 490BC Persia attacks Athens but is defeated at the Battle of Marathon.
- 480BC The second Persian war also leads to defeat for Persia.
- 443–429BC Athens flourishes under its greatest leader, Pericles.
- 431BC The Peloponnesian Wars begin between Athens and Sparta.
- 404BC The Spartans defeat the Athenians.

Hellenistic Age

In 336BC, a young man called Alexander became ruler of the small kingdom of Macedonia, north of Greece. Within just a few years, he and his well trained army had conquered one of the greatest empires of the ancient world. They swept across Asia Minor and marched down the eastern Mediterranean coast to take over Phoenicia (modern Syria) and Judea (modern Palestine). Then they moved on to Egypt, where Alexander was accepted as a child of the Sun God. From there, Alexander and his men went north once more, to take Persia, then the world's greatest empire. Soon Persia too was in Alexander's hands, together with the area of the Indus Valley, on the borders of India. Alexander was preparing to conquer Arabia when he died of a fever, aged only 33.

▲ COIN
The head of Alexander the Great (356–323BC), wearing the horns of an Egyptian god appears on this coin. His exploits gained him almost legendary status.

Alexander was one of the most brilliant generals and powerful leaders the world has known. He was highly educated – his teacher was the Greek philosopher Aristotle – but also a skilled horseman and had boundless energy. After conquering Persia, he would have continued into India but his men were exhausted.

By the time he died, Alexander had journeyed 32,000km/20,000 miles on his epic voyage of conquest. Everywhere he went, he took with him the Greek culture and way of life, so spreading it over a huge area. He founded cities, often called Alexandria after him,

▲ ALEXANDRIAN LIBRARY
The city of Alexandria contained a fabulous library where many of the works of the great Greek writers were preserved on papyrus rolls. The library burned down in AD391.

◀ BUCEPHALUS
Alexander had a preferred horse, Bucephalus. Legend says the horse was wild and only responded to Alexander.

ALEXANDER
When Philip II of Macedonia was killed, Alexander took over a kingdom that was the strongest in Greece. Philip was about to attack Persia when he died. Alexander inherited his ambition.

▶ ALEXANDRIA
The Castle of Qaitbay stands in the present-day city of Alexandria in Egypt. Alexander founded this city in 332BC. He founded others, many of which were named after him.

▲ DELPHIC ORACLE
The Greeks often consulted an oracle for advice before undertaking a momentous event. The most famous was the oracle at Delphi. Philip II and Alexander consulted her.

◂ BATTLE OF ISSUS
At the Battle of Issus, in 333BC, Alexander with a much smaller force defeated the much larger Persian army under Darius III. It was a tremendous victory, opening Syria and Egypt to Alexander's advance.

▾ TIARA
As the Macedonian army swept across Persia, they took what booty they could carry with them. They especially prized Persian metalwork, such as this gold tiara and other items made from gold and silver worn by Persian nobles.

and left behind workers who filled them with classical buildings – temples, theatres, houses, all in the Greek style. For 300 years, this Greek style remained fashionable all over western Asia. Historians now call this period the Hellenistic Age, after Hellas, the Greeks' own name for their country.

Alexander's vast empire did not survive his death. His generals carved it up between them. Ptolemy, ancestor of Queen Cleopatra, ruled Egypt; Antigonous took over Greece and much of Turkey; Seleucus, founder of the Seleucid dynasty of Persian kings, controlled the area from Turkey to the Indus. Only cities named Alexandria remained to remind people of the great general from Macedonia.

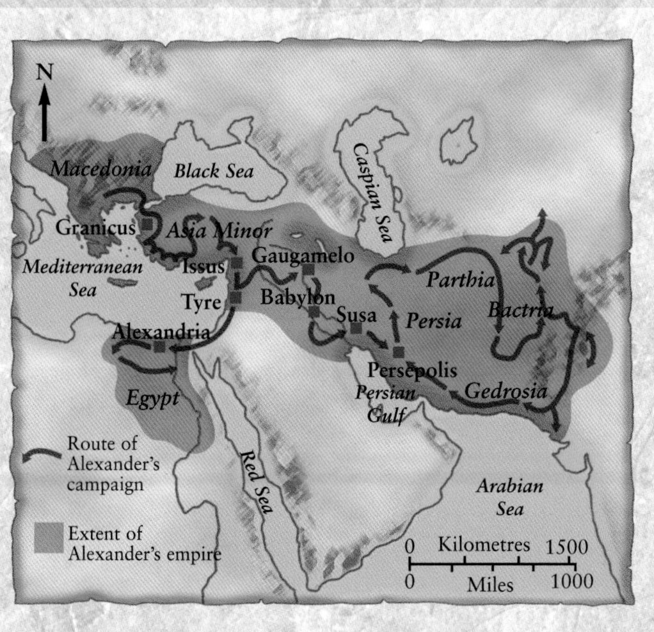

◂ ALEXANDER'S WORLD
The map shows the extent of Alexander's empire and the major routes he took. From its heartland in Greece and the Aegean coast of Turkey, Alexander's empire spread east to the River Indus. The Macedonians founded several Alexandrias in Persia, as well as the more famous one in Egypt.

Key Dates

- 356BC Alexander born in Macedonia.
- 336BC Alexander becomes ruler of Macedonia and puts down uprisings in Greece.
- 333BC Alexander defeats the Persians at the Battle of Issus.
- 332BC Macedonians conquer Egypt. Alexander is accepted as pharaoh.
- 331BC Alexander wins the Battle of Gaugamela, the final defeat of the Persians.
- 326BC Alexander and his army reach the Indus River.
- 323BC Alexander dies of a fever. His empire breaks up.

Ancient Rome

▲ ROMULUS AND REMUS
According to legend, two brothers – Romulus and Remus – founded Rome. Abandoned as babies, they were left to die but a she-wolf suckled them and they survived.

TWO THOUSAND YEARS ago a small Italian town grew to become the most important city in the whole of the western world. The name of the town was Rome. Built on seven hills near the River Tiber, Rome was already powerful by the 3rd century BC. It had a well-organized government, a fearsome army and had taken over the whole of Italy. Over the next 200 years, Rome expanded its influence to become the heart of a great empire. By AD117, the Roman Empire stretched from Britain to North Africa, and from Spain to Palestine.

At the heart of this great empire was the city of Rome itself. At the heart of the city was the forum, a market square surrounded by large public buildings, such as temples, baths and stadiums. The Romans took much from the ancient Greek culture. Many of their public buildings looked similar to Greek ones, with classical pillars and marble sculptures.

Beyond the forum were streets of dwelling places. City land was expensive. Poorer Romans could not afford houses so they rented apartments arranged in multi-level blocks, like modern flats. On the ground floor of each block were shops full of goods and craftworkers. Between the shops was an entrance way, leading to the apartments above. Some had larger, more expensive, rooms. Others, further up the building, were smaller and cheaper. Few had their own water supply or proper kitchen.

In the countryside too, many ordinary Romans lived in poverty, working the land to supply food for the cities. Here, land was cheaper and more plentiful so the wealthiest Romans built themselves large, graceful villas, or country houses. These often had their own baths and an underfloor central heating system.

◀ HUNTING
In the countryside, Romans hunted wild boar with dogs. Hunting provided enjoyment and also gave the Romans a more varied diet.

SOCIETY
Roman society was divided into classes, or social groups. At the top were generals, governors, magistrates and other important officials. Further down were bankers and merchants. Below were craftworkers and shopkeepers. Bottom of the social pile were slaves. Romans were either citizens, free people with rights, or non-citizens.

▼ SHIPS
The Romans used ships for war and trade. Slaves worked to drive them forward by means of banks of oars on either side.

▲ AT THE BATHS
Roman cities had large public bath complexes. There were different rooms with baths of different temperatures, and bathers went from one to the other, finishing up with a cold plunge and an invigorating massage. People went to the baths not only to get clean but also to meet friends and socialize.

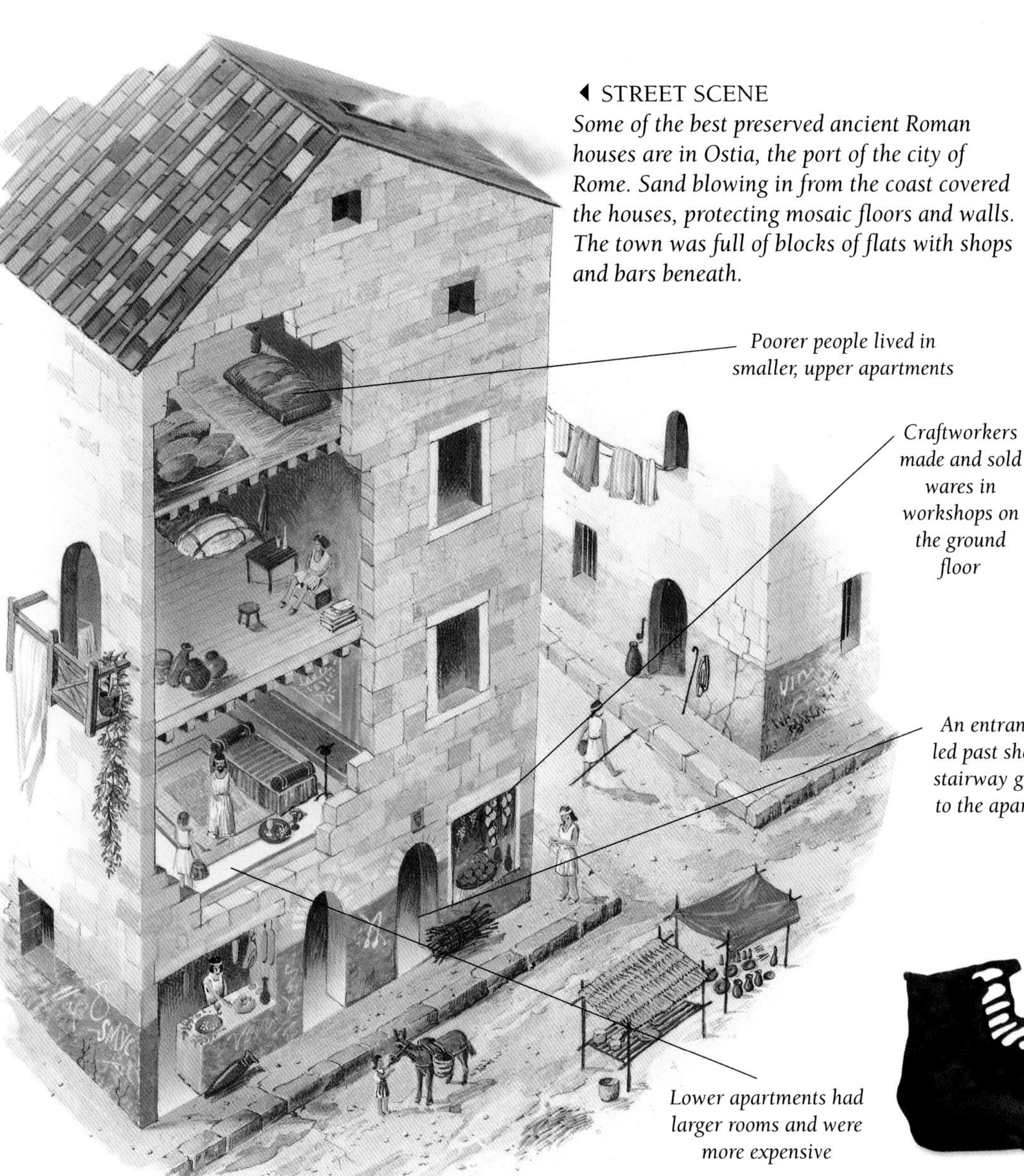

◀ STREET SCENE
Some of the best preserved ancient Roman houses are in Ostia, the port of the city of Rome. Sand blowing in from the coast covered the houses, protecting mosaic floors and walls. The town was full of blocks of flats with shops and bars beneath.

▲ CLOTHING
Most Romans dressed simply and according to class. Outside, Roman citizens only wore a toga, a large piece of white woollen cloth, wound round the body. Roman women wore long linen or woollen tunics.

◀ SHOE
Romans wore leather shoes or sandals, which laced part way up the leg.

▼ NEPTUNE
The Romans worshipped the same gods as the ancient Greeks but gave them different names. The Greek Poseidon, king of the sea, became the Roman Neptune, shown here.

Key Dates

- 753BC According to legend, Rome is founded by Romulus and Remus.
- 509BC Rome becomes a republic.
- 146BC Rome defeats Carthage.
- 58–50BC Julius Caesar conquers Gaul.
- 44BC Julius Caesar is assassinated.
- 27BC Augustus becomes first of the Roman emperors.
- AD117 Emperor Trajan conquers Dacia (Romania). Empire is at its largest extent.
- AD324 Christianity becomes the official religion of the empire.
- AD410 Invading Goths conquer and destroy the city of Rome.

Ancient Rome

As Rome's influence grew, so its government changed. The city had once been ruled by kings but in 509BC, it became a republic, governed by elected consuls. A senate advised the consuls. Under the consuls, Rome's power grew until, by the 2nd century BC, only Carthage, the powerful North African trading empire, could stand up to its might. In 146BC the Romans destroyed Carthage. Rome continued to be a republic until 27BC when, after a civil war, Augustus became the first Roman emperor. For the next 500 years, a series of emperors ruled an empire that was the largest in the western world.

◀ AQUEDUCT
The Romans built many aqueducts to bring in water from the rivers in the countryside to the city. Rome had many aqueducts and was the only ancient city with a reliable water supply. Roman aqueducts still stand today in cities as far apart as Nîmes, France and Istanbul, Turkey.

There were many reasons for Rome's success. The empire had a strong, well-organized army. The Romans also gained rich spoils whenever the army conquered a new territory. In this way, Rome had access to a wide range of raw materials, including iron from central Europe and gold and silver from Spain. As the Romans conquered new territories, they introduced their own system of government, language and laws into the conquered regions.

The empire also included many talented engineers, who built bridges and aqueducts as well as the first large domes. The Romans developed concrete. They also built a huge network of long, straight roads across the empire, linking all parts of the empire to Rome. Many of these routes are still used today.

By AD220, the power of Rome appeared complete. The Romans seemed to be able to build anything and their army seemed to be able to conquer any country. But in the end, the empire became too large. Peoples from the lands on the fringes of the empire in central Europe began to rebel, and it was difficult for the army to move quickly and crush their revolts. Rome's vast empire began to fall apart. In AD395, the empire divided into two and within a few years the last Roman emperor was overthrown.

ROMAN ARMY
Without their powerful army, the Romans would have had no empire. The Roman army conquered new territories and defended frontiers. It also worked on huge engineering projects such as bridges and roads.

◀ LEGIONARY
The best-trained soldiers in the Roman army were the 150,000 legionaries. They were highly disciplined, and wore metal battle dress.

▶ JULIUS CAESAR
Caesar was a consul who ruled Rome as dictator. He conquered Gaul (France) and invaded Britain. His enemies assassinated him in 44BC.

▲ TRAJAN'S COLUMN
Roman legions attack Dacians in this detail from Trajan's Column in Rome. Made of marble, the column was built to the orders of Emperor Trajan, who led a campaign against the Dacians in AD117.

▸ COLOSSEUM
The Roman emperors staged great "games" to win the approval of the Roman people. The Colosseum in Rome, shown here, was the most famous arena. Opened in AD80, it could hold up to 50,000 spectators who crowded in to see gladiators fight.

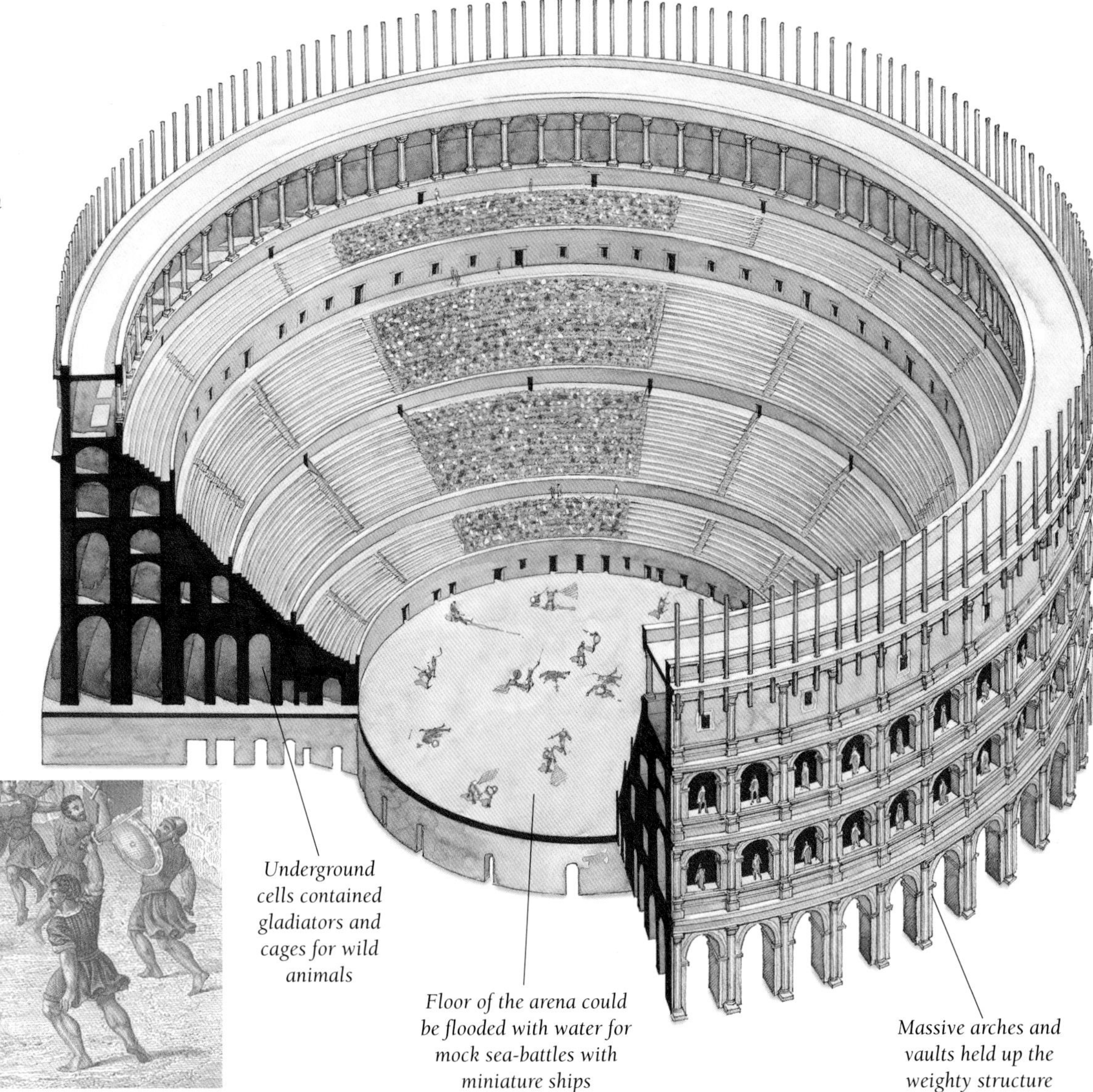

▾ GLADIATOR
Specially trained, gladiators fought each other to the death or were forced into combat with wild beasts from all over the empire. Slaves and prisoners of war were used as gladiators.

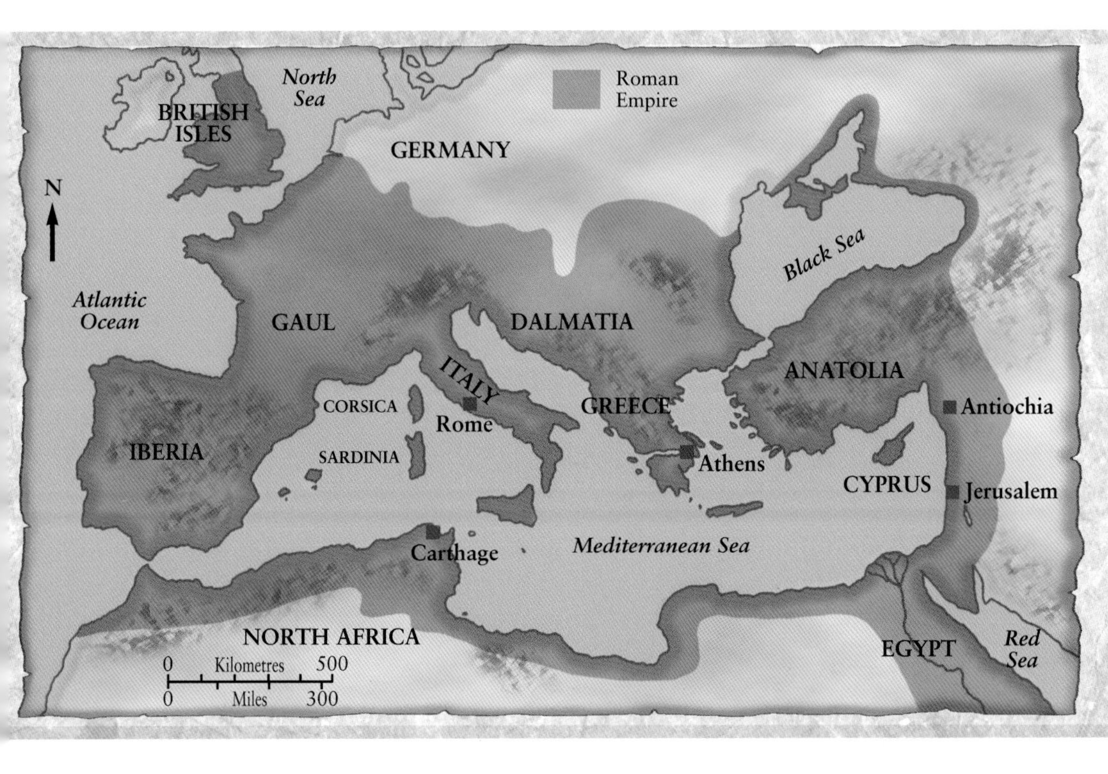

◂ ROMAN EMPIRE
At its largest extent, in around AD117, Rome's empire stretched right across Europe into western Asia. Hadrian's wall, northern England, was the northern frontier. Egypt was the empire's southernmost point. In AD395, the empire, which was too large, divided. The eastern empire became known as the Byzantine Empire.

Early Dynastic China

CIVILIZATION IN CHINA grew up quite separately from the rest of the world. In many ways, Chinese civilization was far in advance of Europe and western Asia, whose people did not know what was happening in China. The Chinese invented many things, including metal working and writing, without any contact with other peoples. This made the Chinese way of life quite distinctive.

Periods of Chinese history are named after dynasties or ruling families. One of the earliest was the Shang dynasty, which began in about 1650BC. Many of the key features of Chinese daily life evolved at this time, such as farming and ancestor worship. The Shang Chinese also became skilled at working in bronze and jade. They developed a form of writing, which later became the written characters still used in China today.

China is a vast country and the Shang dynasty controlled only northern China. The ruling priest-kings were supremely powerful. To the Chinese, they were god-like figures, who could communicate with their ancestors in heaven.

The Shang built many capital cities, possibly

▲ RITUAL VESSEL
This bronze container was used for religious offerings. An ancestor spirit, in the form of a tiger, stands protectively over a man. Other beasts, probably also spirits, cover the tiger's skin.

▶ BRONZE CASTING
Shang Chinese pour molten bronze into a mould. The Chinese had developed bronze casting by about 1650BC and used bronze for making dishes and other items. The king appointed special officials to run the industry.

BELIEFS
The ancient Chinese believed spirits controlled everything. They also worshipped their dead ancestors. One teacher who influenced Chinese beliefs was Confucius. Another was Lao-tze (b. 604BC), founder of Taoism (The Way). This teaches the need to be in harmony with earth, nature and the cosmos.

▶ ORACLE BONE
When a priest wanted to ask ancestor spirits a question, he wrote the question on a piece of bone. He put the bone into the fire until it cracked, then "read" the marks. They were the first form of Chinese writing.

◀ CONFUCIUS
One of the greatest of the Chinese philosophers was Confucius (551-479BC). He taught his followers to help and respect others, to value the family and to respect elders.

◀ YIN AND YANG
Yin and yang symbol. Traditional Chinese beliefs are based on the idea that everything and everyone contains yin – darkness – and yang – lightness. Health and well-being occur when they are balanced.

moving them because of floods from China's great rivers. They built the first at Erlitou, then founded the cities of Zhengzhou and Anyang. Archaeologists have found remains of wooden houses, a palace, storerooms and streets at Anyang. They also found a king's grave. It contained pottery, bronze and jade items, and nearly 4,000 cowrie shells, which the Shang used for money. Also in the tomb were the remains of 47 other people, probably servants sacrificed when their ruler died.

In the 11th century BC, the Zhou dynasty, from north of Anyang, took over from the Shang. The Zhou rulers introduced coins into China and Zhou craftworkers discovered how to work iron. They also invented the crossbow. The Zhou ruled for around 800 years, letting local lords look after their own areas. But the lords began to fight each other. The Zhou dynasty ended and China entered what is known as the Warring States period.

◀ FARMING
For thousands of years the Chinese have farmed the fertile land around the Yellow River, which often floods. The Shang Chinese grew millet, wheat and rice. They also domesticated cattle, pigs, dogs and sheep.

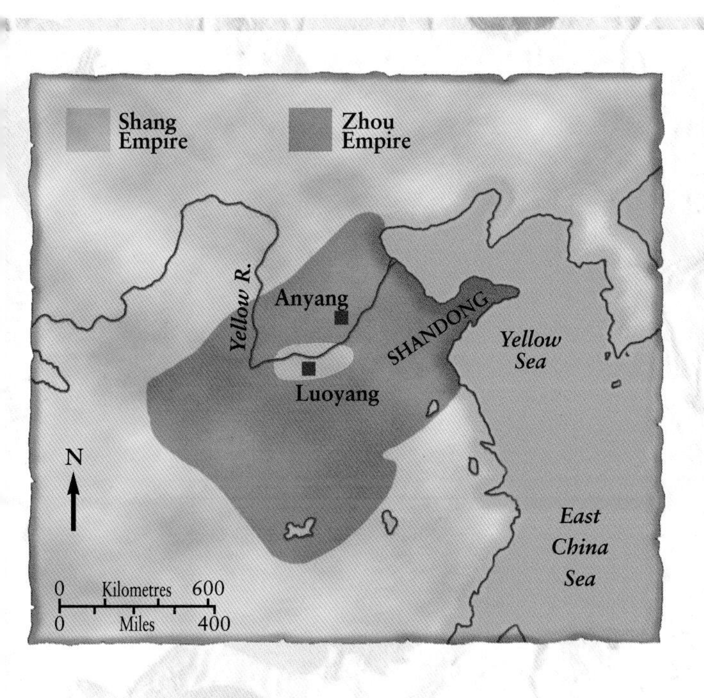

◀ EARLY DYNASTIC CHINA
The map shows the territories of the Shang and Zhou dynasties. The Shang homeland was by the Yellow River, where its waters left the mountains to flow down on to a broad fertile plain. Here they built their main cities – Anyang was a Shang capital. The Zhou came from farther north but also occupied the plain. They made Luoyang their capital city.

Key Dates

- 1650–1027BC Shang dynasty. China's first great Bronze Age civilization develops.
- 1027–256BC Zhou dynasty. The kingdom is divided into many states and the king rules through local lords.
- 481–221BC Warring States period. Local noblemen clash in large-scale battles. China becomes weaker.
- 221BC The first Qin emperor unifies China.

Qin China

▲ LUCKY DRAGON
The dragon was a Qin symbol of good luck. When he came to the throne, Qin Shi Huang made the creature his own symbol. Ever since, the emperor, the dragon, and the idea of good fortune have been linked closely in China.

BY THE THIRD century BC, war had torn China apart. Seven different states fought each other. For years, no state was strong enough to win a decisive victory and take control of China. Then, in 221BC, the armies of Qin defeated their enemies and brought the seven states together under their leader, Zheng. He took the title Qin Shi Huang, the First Sovereign Emperor of Qin.

The First Emperor ruled for only 11 years. But the changes he made lasted much longer and helped later dynasties, such as the Han and Yüan, to rule effectively. His empire was so large, and contained people of so many different backgrounds, that Zheng had to be ruthless to keep China united. Troops executed anyone who disagreed with his policies. They also burned books by writers who disagreed with the emperor.

Another way of making this huge country easier to govern was to create national systems that all people could use. The First Emperor ordered that everyone in China should use the same systems of weights, measurements and writing. He also began a policy of building roads and canals, so his officials and merchants could travel easily around the country.

The Xiongnu, a nomadic people from the north of China, were always threatening to invade. So the emperor built the Great Wall to keep out the invaders. He ordered his builders to join up many existing walls along China's northern frontier. Working on the wall

▲ TERRACOTTA ARMY
The First Emperor's tomb contained 7,500 life-size terracotta models of the emperor's army, from foot soldiers and crossbowmen to charioteers and officers. Each was based on a real-life soldier. Automatic crossbows were placed by the entrance to fire if anyone tried to rob the tomb.

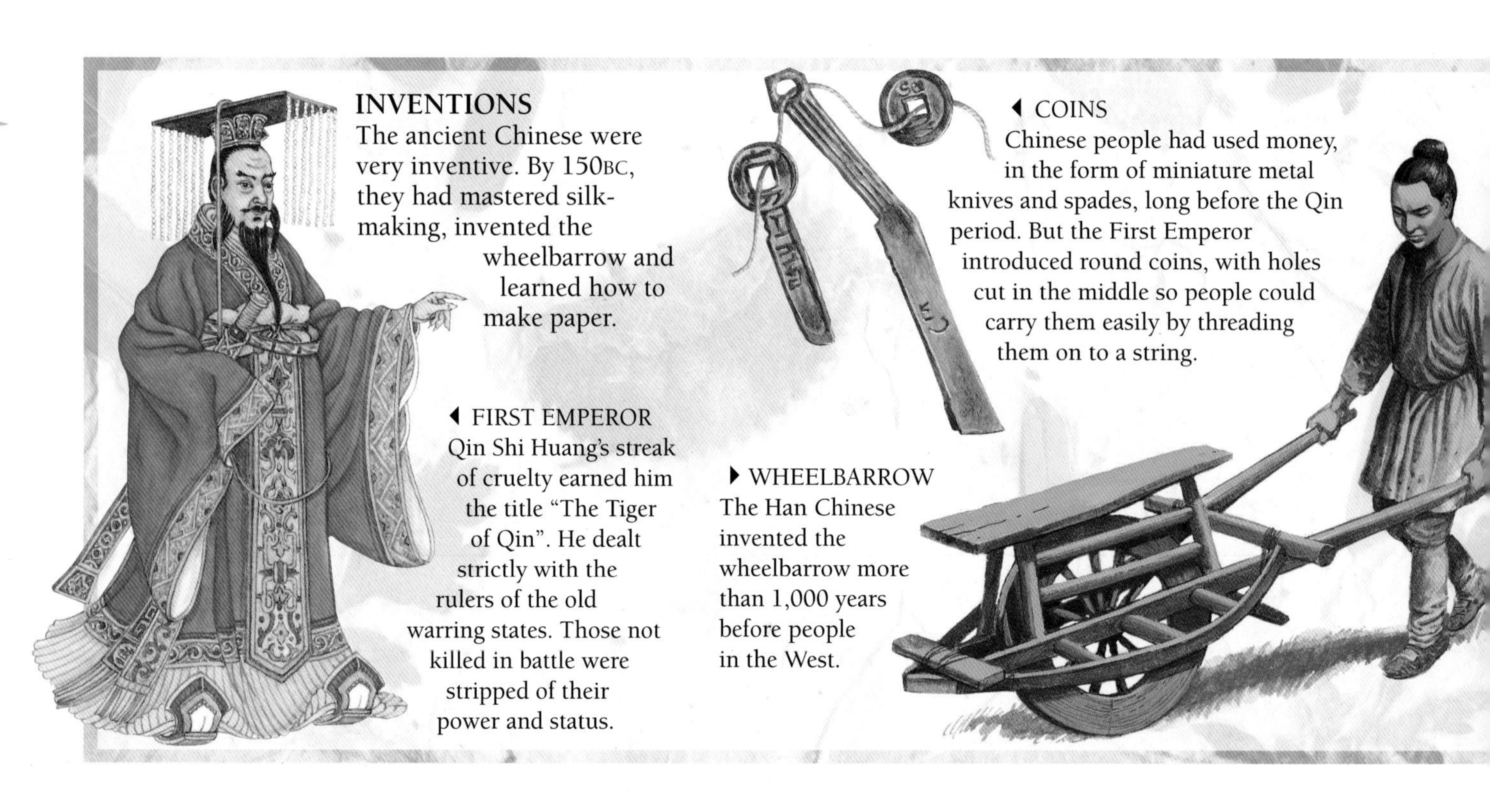

INVENTIONS
The ancient Chinese were very inventive. By 150BC, they had mastered silk-making, invented the wheelbarrow and learned how to make paper.

◀ FIRST EMPEROR
Qin Shi Huang's streak of cruelty earned him the title "The Tiger of Qin". He dealt strictly with the rulers of the old warring states. Those not killed in battle were stripped of their power and status.

◀ COINS
Chinese people had used money, in the form of miniature metal knives and spades, long before the Qin period. But the First Emperor introduced round coins, with holes cut in the middle so people could carry them easily by threading them on to a string.

▶ WHEELBARROW
The Han Chinese invented the wheelbarrow more than 1,000 years before people in the West.

▲ GREAT WALL
Today the Great Wall stretches around 6,300km/3,900 miles in length. It is the longest structure ever created by humans.

was hazardous. For much of its length, the wall ran through mountains. It was exhausting work carrying stone and moving earth to create ramparts. Many workers died. Other people suffered because they had to pay high taxes for the wall.

Qin Shi Huang worked hard to keep his empire together. After his death, war caused the empire to break up for a while.

◀ BUILDING THE GREAT WALL
The Great Wall was built as a solid obstacle against invasions. It was also a communications network. Officers would signal to each other using bonfires, and messengers could ride along the top of the wall.

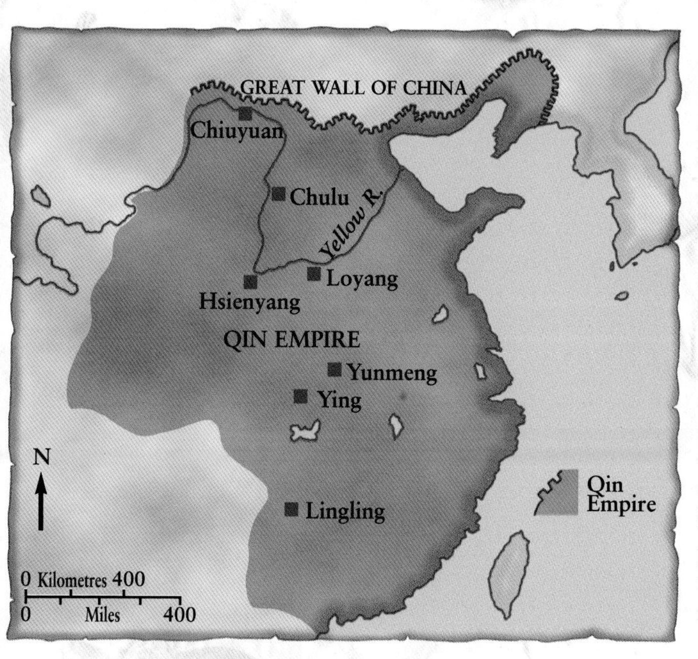

◀ QIN EMPIRE
The map shows the extent of the Qin Empire. From the heartlands along the banks of the Yellow River, the empire of the Qin stretched north to the fort at Juyan, south to Panyu (near modern Canton), and west into the province of Sichuan. Qin is pronounced chin, the origin of the name China.

Key Dates

- 246BC Zheng becomes ruler of the kingdom of Qin.
- 230-222BC A series of victories brings the armies of Qin control of most of the warring states.
- 221BC Qin defeats the last of the warring states. Zheng becomes the First Emperor.
- 213BC The First Emperor orders books by authors opposing his rule to be burned.
- 210BC Qin Shi Huang dies.
- 209–208BC A peasant rebellion reduces the power of the Qin government.
- 207BC Qin empire breaks up.

Han China

▲ BRONZE HORSE
This beautiful bronze horse was made nearly 2000 years ago by skilled Chinese craftworkers.

THE PERIOD OF THE Chinese Han dynasty was a time of exciting change. Technology and industry improved, farming became more efficient, and Chinese merchants traded along routes that stretched right across the huge continent of Asia. These developments were so wide-reaching that even today, many Chinese people think of the Han period as the true beginning of China.

The Han emperors took over the government of the Qin dynasty. They organized China into a series of local provinces, each with its own commander. The Qin dynasty had ruled by force but the Han emperors found more peaceful ways of wielding their power. When Han ironworkers discovered how to increase the temperature of their furnaces, they were able to make a much wider range of better quality products. The emperors saw the value of this and put all the iron foundries under state ownership. This gave them control of all the tools and weapons that were produced.

The emperors also tried to control trade, especially the rich trade in silk, which Chinese merchants carried along the overland routes across central Asia. Nearby areas were only allowed to trade with China if they paid regular tribute to the emperor.

▲ MEASURING EARTHQUAKES
This wonderful object was used to detect earthquakes. The slightest tremor loosened a trigger in a dragon's jaw. The jaw opened, releasing a ball into a frog's mouth below.

◀ EXAMINATIONS
Emperor Wu Di (r.140–87BC) thought of the first civil service exams. He founded a special university where candidates could study the writings of Confucius, which they had to learn by heart in order to pass their exams.

CIVIL SERVICE
The first Han emperor, Gaozu (r. 206–195BC) was not highly educated, but he knew he needed well qualified officials to run his empire. He started the civil service with a small group of scholars, who recruited more and more officials.

▶ GOOD MARKS
The circles on this 19th-century Chinese exam paper indicate where the tutor thought the student's calligraphy was particularly good.

The Han emperors also set up a civil service to administer the empire. They created a huge number of officials, who got their jobs by taking an examination. Candidates had to answer questions on the teachings of the philosopher Confucius. This civil service, with its system of examinations, lasted some 2,000 years – much longer than the Han dynasty itself.

The most important of all the changes that took place under the Han emperors were in technology. Paper and fine porcelain, or china, were both Han inventions. Scientists of the Han period even made the world's first seismograph for predicting earthquakes. They also invented a water clock, the wheelbarrow and the stern-post rudder, for better steering of boats at sea. At the same time, merchants brought many new materials into China, from wool and furs to glass and pearls. Peaceful and wealthy, Han China was probably the most advanced civilization of its time.

▶ PRECIOUS SILK
The Chinese used silk for kimonos, wall hangings and, before the Han invented paper and ink, even as a writing material. Silk making began in China some 4,000 years ago. The Chinese kept the details of its production secret and earned a huge income from trading in the luxurious fabric.

▼ THE JADE PRINCESS
This body of a Han princess, wrapped in jade, dates back from the 1st century BC. *The Chinese believed jade was magical. They thought it would preserve anything wrapped in it for ever.*

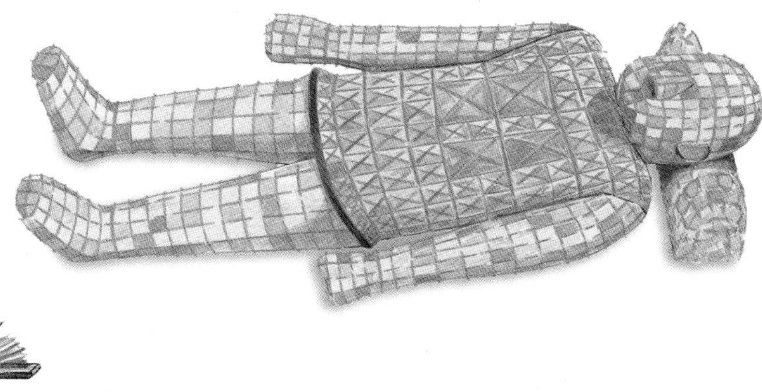

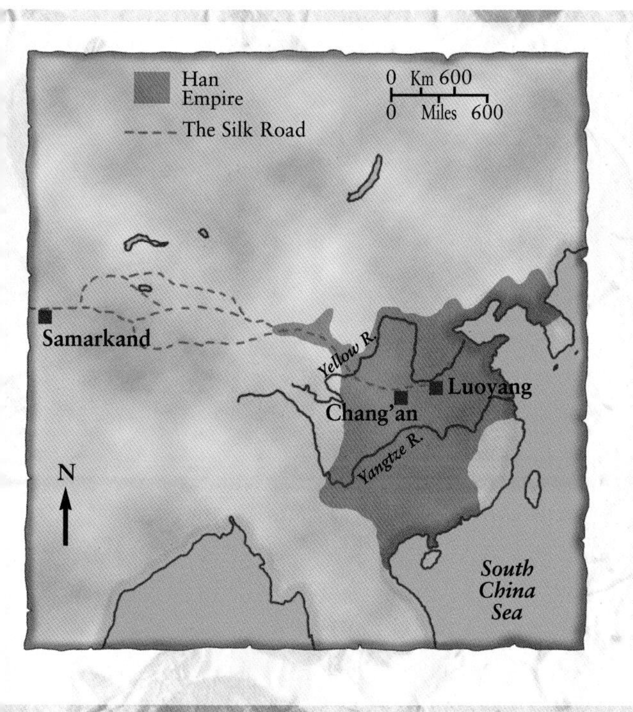

◀ HAN EMPIRE
The Han empire stretched far into the northwest, along the routes of the silk merchants into central Asia. The Han emperors also pushed into the south, where population increased towards the end of the Han period. The earliest Han capital city, and site of the imperial palace, was at Chang'an. Later the capital moved to Luoyang.

Key Dates

- 207BC Gaozu overthrows the Qin dynasty. The Han dynasty rules from the city of Chang'an.
- 140–87BC The reign of Han Wu Di. He defeats the northern nomads. The Han empire reaches its largest extent.
- 124BC Competitive examinations for the civil service begin.
- 119BC Iron industry nationalized.
- AD25 Later Han period begins. The emperor moves the capital to Luoyang.
- AD105 An official called Cai Lun develops the paper-making process.
- AD220 Power struggles weaken the court and the Han empire collapses.

Early Japan

▲ POTTERY FIGURINE
Jomon potters showed their skill making figurines like this.

FOR THOUSANDS OF YEARS after the last Ice Age, the people of Japan survived by hunting and gathering. Archaeologists call these early people the Jomon. They used tools made of stone and bone and by about 10,500BC, had produced some of the world's first pottery, even though they did not use the potter's wheel.

During the 3rd century BC, a new people arrived in Japan, probably from the mainland of Asia. Known as the Yayoi, they were the first people in Japan to grow rice in irrigated fields. They also brought metal working to Japan as well as domesticated animals, woven cloth and the potter's wheel, and established a new, settled agricultural society.

The Yayoi people began farming rice on the southern Japanese island of Kyushu. Soon their farming way of life had spread to much of Japan's main island, Honshu. Yayoi farmers used stone tools, such as reaping knives, and made hoes and spades out of wood. Bronze was used mainly for weapons and finely decorated

◀ FARMING RICE
Early Japanese cultivated rice in wet paddy fields. Rice farming probably came to Japan from Korea between 500 and 300BC.

IMPORTED SKILLS
Settlers who came from mainland Asia brought important skills to early Japan. These were bronze and iron casting, useful for making effective tools. They also brought the potter's wheel, so the Japanese could make earthenware objects like jugs and pots, and they introduced land irrigation for growing rice.

◀ BRONZE BELL
Bells like this, covered with decorative patterns and simple pictures of humans and animals, were made in both the Yayoi and Yamato periods. Unlike western bells, they did not have clappers, so must have been rung by beating.

▲ GONE FISHING
Japanese fishermen pursue a whale through high seas in this typically stylized image. Early people in northeastern Japan relied on fish and other seafood for much of their diet. Whale meat was an important food source to them.

▼ TOMB HORSE
When a Yamato emperor died, the people surrounded his burial site with thousands of pottery objects, such as this horse. They were meant to protect the tomb and its contents.

◀ SHINTO
A Shinto temple in Nikko, Japan. Shinto is the traditional religion of Japan. It dates back to very early Japan and was based on a love of nature and belief in spirits, called kami.

items such as bells and mirrors. From this evidence, archaelogists believe that only rich or high-status Japanese, such as chiefs, priests and warriors, used metal items. Their owners may have used many of these bronze items, including bells, in ceremonies to celebrate the passing of the seasons or rituals performed during rice planting and harvesting.

By the 3rd century AD, some of the warrior-chiefs had gained power over large areas of Japan. These powerful families became the leaders of the next Japanese culture, the Yamato. They claimed to be descended from the sun goddess and their power soon stretched across the whole of Japan. They led their soldiers on horseback, and copied the government of the Chinese emperors, with large courts and ranks of officials. The Yamato built hill-top settlements to defend themselves and huge burial tombs, surrounded by moats, were also used for protection. These tombs, filled with adornments and weapons, indicate the great power and wealth of the Yamato emperors.

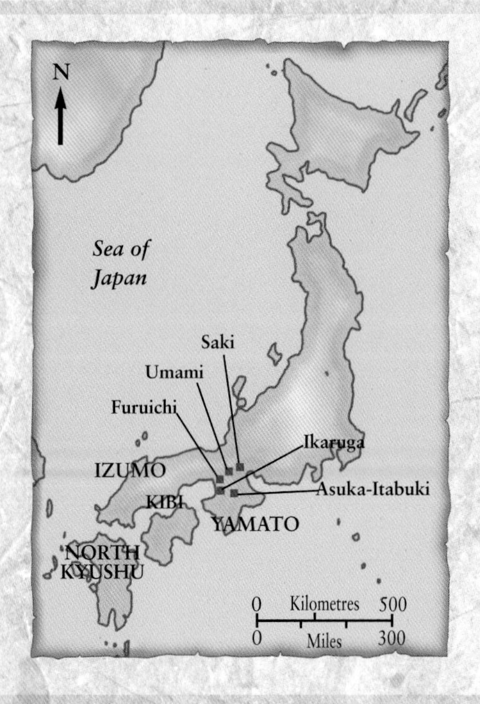

◀ EARLY JAPAN
The Yayoi rice farmers spread northwards from southern Japan. They are named after the section of modern Tokyo where remains of their culture were found. The later Yamato culture began on the Yamato plain in southeastern Honshu. The greatest number of Yamato remains, especially palaces and tombs, is still to be found in this area.

Key Dates

- 8000BC Jomon culture of hunter-gatherers dominates Japan.
- 200BC The Yayoi people begin to introduce rice farming.
- AD250 Rise of the Yamato culture.
- AD350 The Yamato emperor rules the whole of Japan.
- AD538 The first Buddhists to settle in Japan arrive from Korea.
- AD604 After a period of weakness, Prince Shotoku Taishi strengthens imperial power and introduces new forms of government based on Chinese models.
- AD710 The Yamato period ends and the state capital moves to the city of Nara.

The Khmers

▲ GLAZED JAR
This Vietnamese jar was made around the 11th century AD. *It has a finely cracked cream glaze, decorated with brown leaf sprays.*

Deep in the jungles of Cambodia stand the remains of some of the largest temples and palaces ever constructed. They are reminders of the great civilization of the Khmers, who flourished between the 9th and 15th centuries AD, and were ruled by kings so powerful that their people believed them to be gods.

The Khmers lived in a difficult, inhospitable part of the world. Dense tropical forests covered much of their country and every year the monsoons flooded their rivers, making it difficult to grow crops. But they began to clear the forests and adapted to the rains, growing rice in the flooded plains on either side of the great Mekong River.

As time went on, the Khmers learned how to dig canals and reservoirs, to drain away and store the flood water. Then they could water their fields during the rest of the year, when there was little rain.

While their farmers were busy in the fields, the Khmers were opening up trade routes through Siam (Thailand) into India. As a result of these links, Khmer artists and architects copied Indian styles, and the Khmers began to adopt the Hindu religion.

▲ ANGKOR WAT
The greatest of all the Khmer temples was Angkor Wat. Started by King Suryavarman II in 1113, it covers a vast area. It contains several courtyards lined with shrines and topped with huge towers. The picture shows a detail from the Elephant's Terrace.

RELIGIOUS TEMPLE
The Khmer kingdom lasted for 500 years. Angkor Wat was its most fabulous achievement. The Khmers were Hindus, who believed in gods such as Vishnu, Shiva and Brahma. Their images appear in reliefs all over the temple. Also at Angkor Wat were statues of Nagas, mythical seven-headed snakes. The Khmers believed they were kindly water spirits.

▶ ANGKOR CARVING
The sculptors who worked at Angkor Wat created fabulous work. This intricate stone carving forms part of a massive gateway to the temple. It has survived for hundreds of years in the Cambodian jungles.

▲ ASPARAS
Carved in relief on the walls and in the courtyard of Angkor Wat, these dancing women were known as *asparas*. Covered in jewels and wearing towering headdresses, they entertained kings.

◀ CUTTING TREES
The Khmers had to clear large areas of tropical forest for farming and to build their temples. They used elephants to move and carry heavy trees. They also used elephants in warfare.

The godly status of the Khmer kings gave them enormous power and made most people eager to work for them. From the 12th century onwards, the kings began enormous building projects – temples covering many acres, surrounded by huge lakes and long canals. Thousands of workers, toiling in groups of 25 or more, hauled massive blocks of stone through the forest to the building sites to create towering temples. They also built hospitals, reservoirs and roads.

The Khmer kingdom lasted until the 15th century, although the people had to fight off several invasion attempts by rival nations jealous of their wealth. Finally, in 1431, an invading army from Siam proved too strong for the Khmers, who fled to a small area in the south of the country.

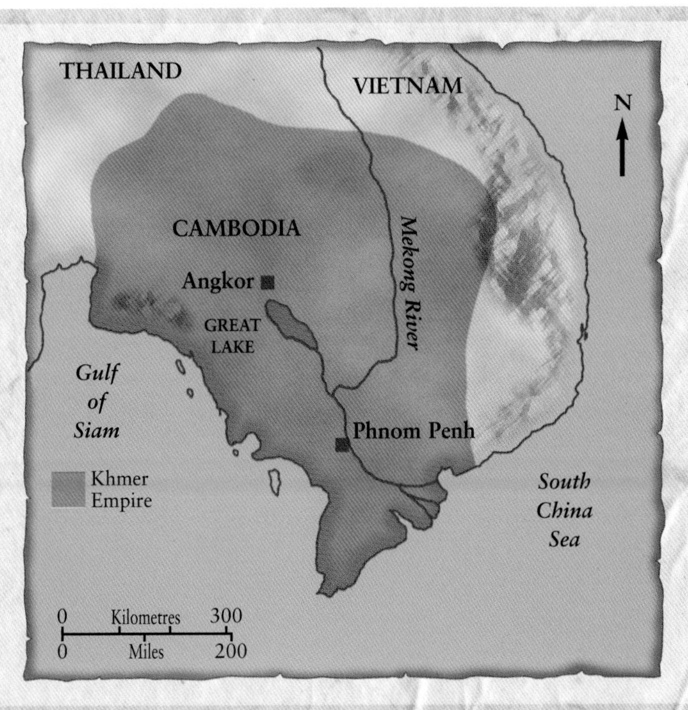

◀ KHMERS
The kingdom of the Khmers occupied much of modern Cambodia, plus the southern part of Vietnam. Around one million people lived in and around the capital, Angkor. The rest of the population occupied the floodplains of rivers such as the Mekong.

Key Dates

- AD802 The Khmer empire is founded under King Jayavarman II (r.802–850).
- AD881 King Yasovarman I builds the earliest surviving Khmer temple.
- AD1113 Work starts on building Angkor Wat.
- AD1177 The Cham sail up the Mekong River and attack Angkor Wat.
- AD1200 King Jayavarman VII builds a new temple, Angkor Thom.
- AD1431 Siamese invaders destroy Angkor; the Khmer empire collapses.

North American Civilizations

THE EARLY CIVILIZATIONS of North America are famous for their burial mounds, remains of which still exist today. These huge structures contain thousands of tons of earth. Large numbers of people must have worked hard for months or even years to build them. The most famous of the North American civilizations were the Hopewell people, who were based in the Ohio River valley, and the mound builders of the Mississippi area.

Hopewell mounds were gathered together in groups. At Hopewell itself, 38 mounds form a complex of 45 hectares/110 acres. Most are round or rectangular mounds. They contain several bodies. The Hopewell people left offerings and belongings in the graves with their dead. These included tools, beads, jewels and ornaments.

Some of the graves were made from raw materials that came from far away because the Hopewells traded over long distances. They imported sea shells from Florida, obsidian (a naturally occurring form of glass) from the Rockies, and flint from Illinois. In return they made goods such as pipes, pottery figurines and copper ornaments as far as southeastern Canada.

After about AD400, the Hopewell trading network began to break down, and the civilization went into decline. No one knows why this happened. Perhaps the population was too large for the local food supply. The climate became colder which may also have cut down the food supply.

But by this time another mound-building group were living in the Mississippi area. They mainly lived in small settlements but created a large city, of perhaps 30,000 people, at Cahokia. This city consisted mainly

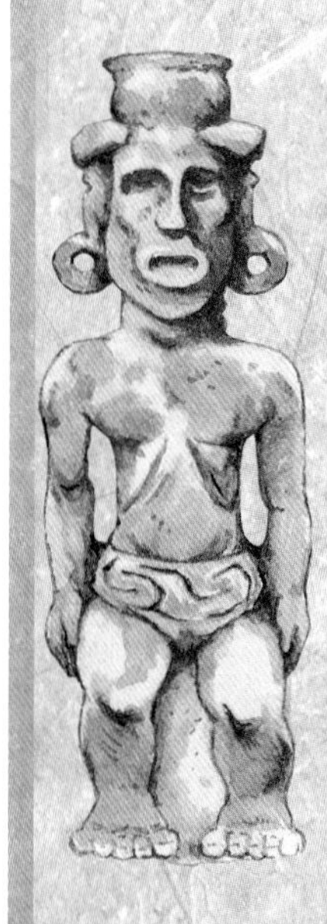

CROPS
The most important crop for the early North American civilizations was maize. Together with beans and squash, it may have come into North America from Mexico. Most early North Americans relied on agriculture, which enabled them to create more permanent settlements.

◀ STONE PIPE
Native Americans may have used this carved stone pipe, dated about 100BC, to smoke various plants, including tobacco. Archaeologists found the pipe in Ohio.

▼ HOMES
Houses made from a framework of wooden poles, covered with thatch, provided homes for early Native Americans in the river valleys of southeastern North America.

▲ MASK
The Kwakiutl, Native Americans from the northwest Pacific coast, carved this elaborate mask. Unlike the Ohio peoples, they relied mainly on fishing for their food.

of wood and thatch houses on the fertile river flood plain. In the central area were more than 100 earth mounds. The largest was the vast Monk's Mound, which was 30m/100ft high and topped by a wood and thatch temple. Cahokia was probably the home of local chiefs, whose period of greatest power lasted some 200 years, from 1050 to 1250AD.

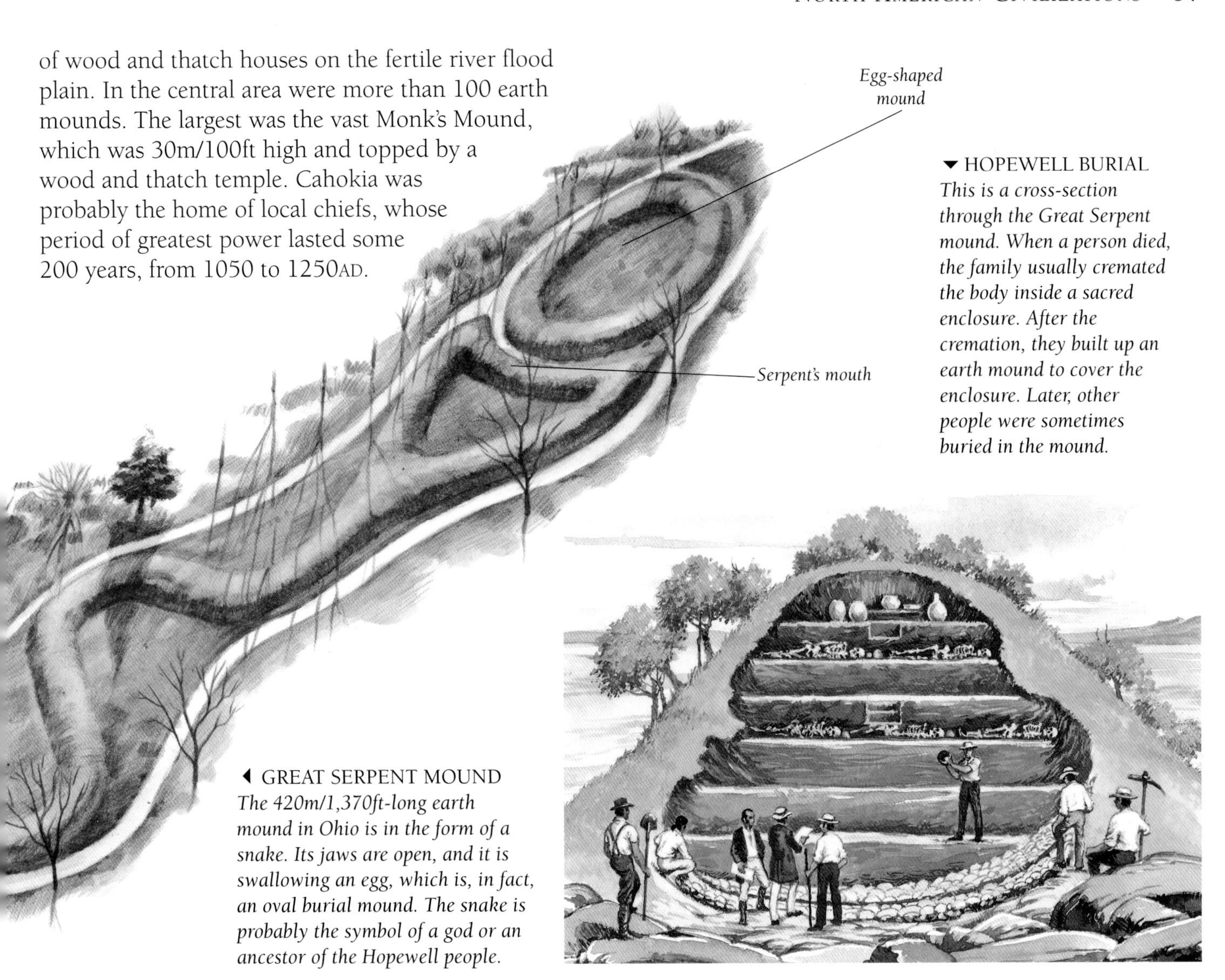

▼ HOPEWELL BURIAL
This is a cross-section through the Great Serpent mound. When a person died, the family usually cremated the body inside a sacred enclosure. After the cremation, they built up an earth mound to cover the enclosure. Later, other people were sometimes buried in the mound.

◀ GREAT SERPENT MOUND
The 420m/1,370ft-long earth mound in Ohio is in the form of a snake. Its jaws are open, and it is swallowing an egg, which is, in fact, an oval burial mound. The snake is probably the symbol of a god or an ancestor of the Hopewell people.

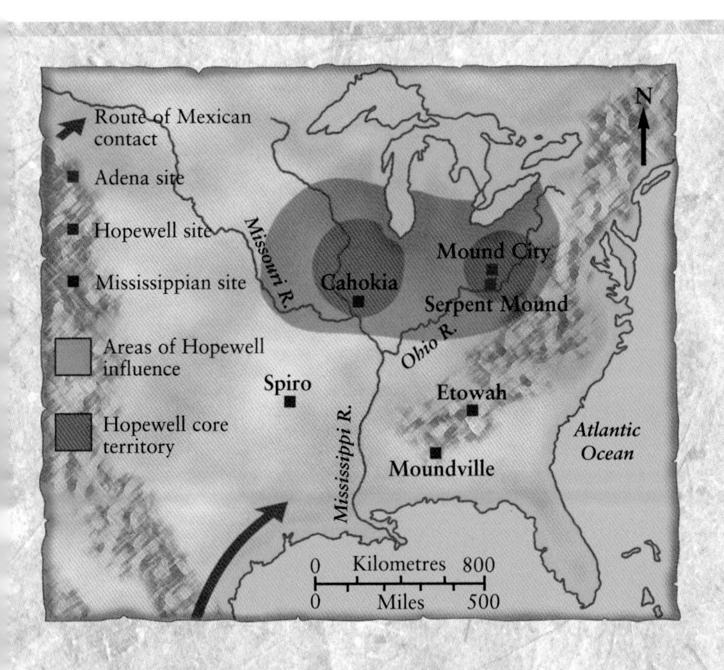

◀ NORTH AMERICA
The Hopewell people had their main areas in Ohio and Illinois. The Mississippi people came from the area where the Mississippi and Missouri rivers joined. But the influence of both peoples spread much farther. Archaeologists have found their goods all over eastern North America, from Florida in the South to Canada in the North.

Key Dates

- 200BC Beginnings of Hopewell civilization.
- AD400 Hopewell civilization declines.
- AD400–800 Maize growing spreads across southeastern North America.
- AD900 Rise of the Mississippi civilization.
- AD1050–1250 Cahokia is a major region of Mississippi civilization.
- AD1250 Power shifts to Moundville, west-central Alabama.

People of the Andes

▲ STAFF GOD
This 4m/13ft-high image, part human, part jaguar, stood in the Castillo, the main temple at Chavín de Huantar.

IT SEEMS AN UNLIKELY PLACE to settle. The high Andes mountains make travel, building and farming difficult. But in the 12th century BC, a group of people started to build cities and ritual areas in these harsh conditions. We know these people as the Chavín, after their city at Chavín de Huantar. During their most prosperous period, their settlements spread for many miles along the coastal plain.

At Chavín, near the Mosna River, they built a large temple complex with a maze of corridors and rooms. Here they hid the images of their gods, who were often beings that combined human and animal features – jaguars, eagles, and snakes. Archaeologists think that people came to the temple to ask the gods about the future, and that priests inside the hidden rooms replied by blowing conch-shell trumpets.

The Chavín were powerful for around 500 years, after which several local cultures sprang up in the region. The Huari people took over much of the Chavín's territory and a civilization of sun-worshippers emerged at Tiahuanaco, Bolivia.

▲ GATEWAY OF THE SUN
The Gateway of the Sun stood at the entrance to the temple at Tiahuanaco, near Lake Titicaca, Bolivia. It was carved out of one enormous piece of stone.

TIAHUANACO
The Tiahuanaco civilization emerged near Lake Titicaca, where they built an extraordinary city and temple complex. On the shores of the lake, the Tiahuanaco people drained large areas of marsh to make farmland to feed the city's population. With the Huari, they controlled the Andes region.

◀ ANIMAL POT
Tiahuanaco's potters were some of the most skilled in South America. They made many of their pots in animal shapes.

▲ TEMPLE WALL
The main buildings at Tiahuanaco included a huge temple whose walls were decorated with stone heads. Tiahuanaco was probably also a bustling city as well as an important ceremonial site.

◀ JAGUAR CULT
Fearsome deities appear in all early Central American civilizations. The jaguar was especially sacred.

The Olmec

THEY WERE KNOWN AS THE PEOPLE of the jaguar. The Olmec came from a small area by the Bay of Campeche in central Mexico. Like the Chavín of South America they worshipped gods that were half-human and half-animal. A jaguar figure seems to have been their preferred, and most feared, deity.

The Olmec were the ancestors of the later Mexican civilizations, such as the Maya and Toltec. Like them, the Olmec cleared the tropical forest to farm maize, squash, beans and tomatoes. Like them too, they built their temples on tall pyramids, expressed their beliefs in stone carvings, and were a strong warlike people.

But the Olmec did not use warfare to build a large empire. They probably used their army to protect the extensive trade links they set up in Central America. This trade brought them a plentiful supply of raw materials, especially rocks such as basalt, jade and obsidian. Olmec sculptors used these materials to produce massive carved heads and decorative reliefs showing their gods.

◀ COLOSSAL HEAD *Archaeologists have found huge heads, such as this, at many Olmec sites. About 1.5m/5ft tall and carved from a single piece of rock, they were probably portraits of Olmec rulers. Olmec sculptors also used precious materials such as jade to carve human heads.*

◀ JAGUAR SPIRIT *The image of the jaguar spirit appeared on all sorts of Olmec objects, such as this pot.*

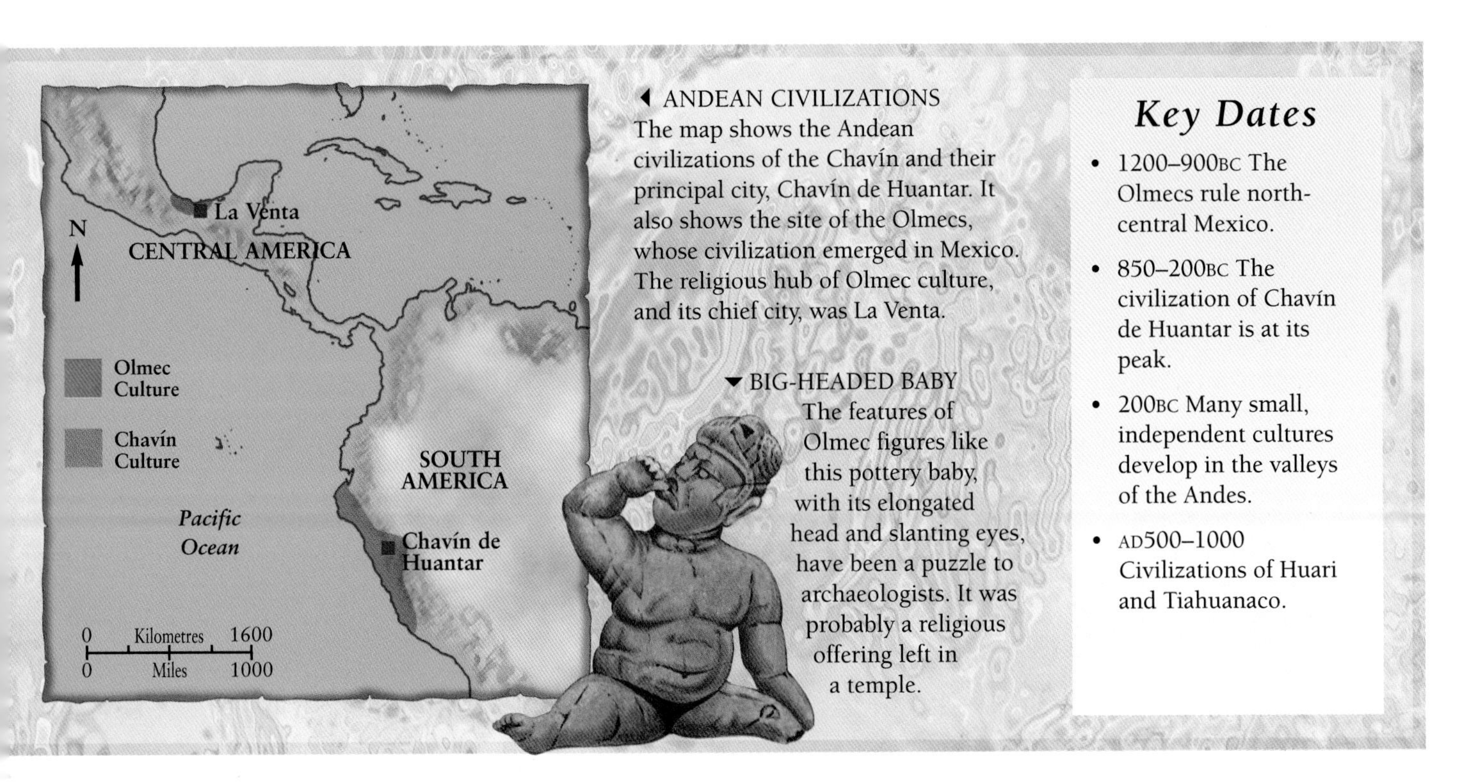

◀ ANDEAN CIVILIZATIONS The map shows the Andean civilizations of the Chavín and their principal city, Chavín de Huantar. It also shows the site of the Olmecs, whose civilization emerged in Mexico. The religious hub of Olmec culture, and its chief city, was La Venta.

▼ BIG-HEADED BABY The features of Olmec figures like this pottery baby, with its elongated head and slanting eyes, have been a puzzle to archaeologists. It was probably a religious offering left in a temple.

Key Dates

- 1200–900BC The Olmecs rule north-central Mexico.
- 850–200BC The civilization of Chavín de Huantar is at its peak.
- 200BC Many small, independent cultures develop in the valleys of the Andes.
- AD500–1000 Civilizations of Huari and Tiahuanaco.

The Maya

▲ CHAC
One of the most important of the many Maya gods was Chac, the god of rain.

DURING THE 19TH century, archaeologists in Mexico were amazed when they stumbled across tall, stone-built, pyramid-shaped temples and broad plazas. They belonged to the Maya, an ancient Mexican people. The Maya created wonderful cities and were scholars. They invented their own system of writing and were skilled in mathematics and astronomy. But they were also a violent people. Their cities were continuously at war with each other. They took prisoners, who were later sacrificed to their gods.

The Maya lived in Mexico before 2000BC. But their cities became large and powerful much later, after AD300, in what historians call the "Classic" phase of their civilization. They developed efficient farming, producing maize, squash, beans and root vegetables to feed their rising population of city-dwellers.

By the Classic period, some Maya cities were huge, holding up to 50,000 people. The people lived in mud-brick houses around the outer edges of the cities. Most of the houses had only one or two rooms, and little in the way of furniture – just thin reed mats to sit on and slightly thicker mats for mattresses.

The chief Maya cities included Palenque, Copan, Tikal and Chichen Itza. In the heart of each of the cities was a complex of pyramid-shaped temples. The Maya continually rebuilt these temple-pyramids, adding more earth and stone to make them larger and taller.

The Maya survived for hundreds of years, but eventually constant civil war ate away at their wealth and power. Chichen Itza declined around 1200 and by the 16th century AD, when the Spanish conquered Mexico, only a few small Maya towns were left.

▲ TIKAL
Tikal was one of the largest cities of the Mayan civilization. Its ruins lie in the tropical rainforest of what is now northern Guatemala.

CRAFTS AND SKILLS

The Maya were skilled craftworkers. They produced fine pottery, carved stone reliefs and jade ornaments. They used razor-sharp flints for stone carving. Some flints were highly decorative and therefore buried as offerings to their gods.

◀ COSTUME
A Maya warrior wears a distinctive headpiece and carries a wooden spear. The Maya wove cloth from plant fibres such as cotton, and used plants to produce decorative dyes.

▼ CODEX
The Maya developed a series of picture symbols for writing, called glyphs. They carved these on stone tablets and also wrote them in books, called codices, made of paper, cloth or animal skins. They were the first Americans to develop picture writing.

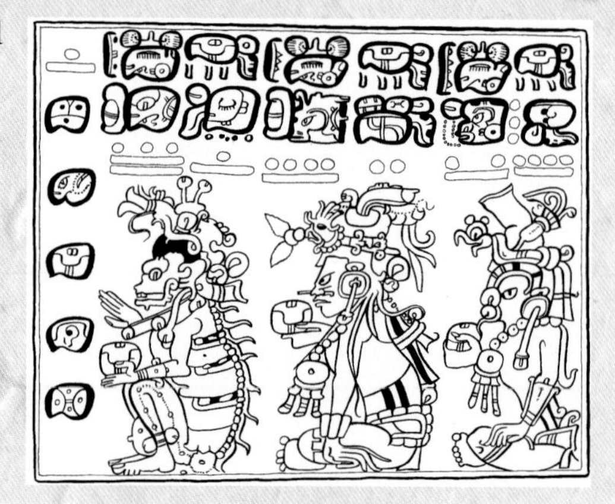

▲ CALENDAR
Astronomers and mathematicians, the Maya also invented calendars. One was a solar calendar, like ours, based on 365 days in the year. The other had a year of 200 days and was used for religious ceremonies.

▲ WALL OF SKULLS
These carvings come from a 60m/200ft-long wall at Chichen Itza. The wall once supported a fence on which heads of sacrificial victims were displayed, skewered on poles.

▲ WARRIOR
The people of Chichen Itza had an army of warriors who were feared all over the Yucatan peninsula. Their prisoners of war were often sacrificed to the gods.

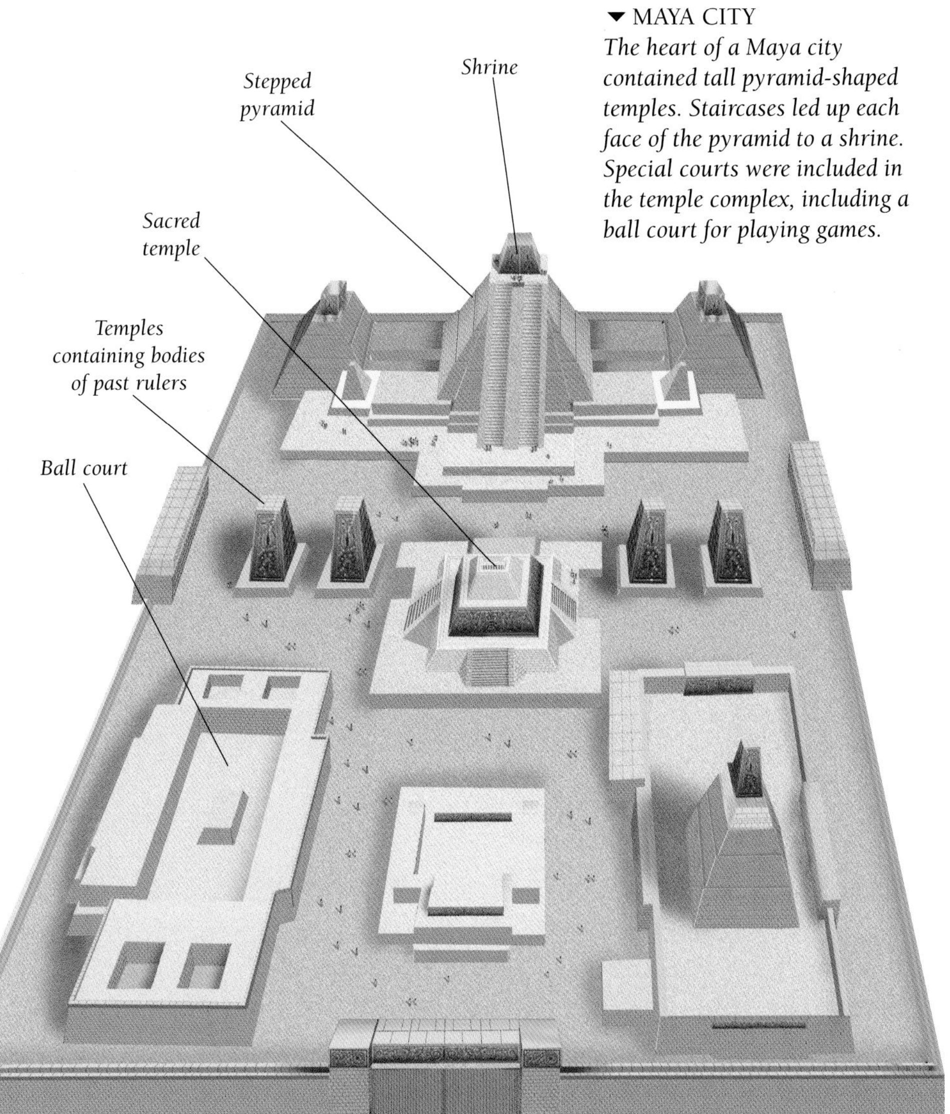

▼ MAYA CITY
The heart of a Maya city contained tall pyramid-shaped temples. Staircases led up each face of the pyramid to a shrine. Special courts were included in the temple complex, including a ball court for playing games.

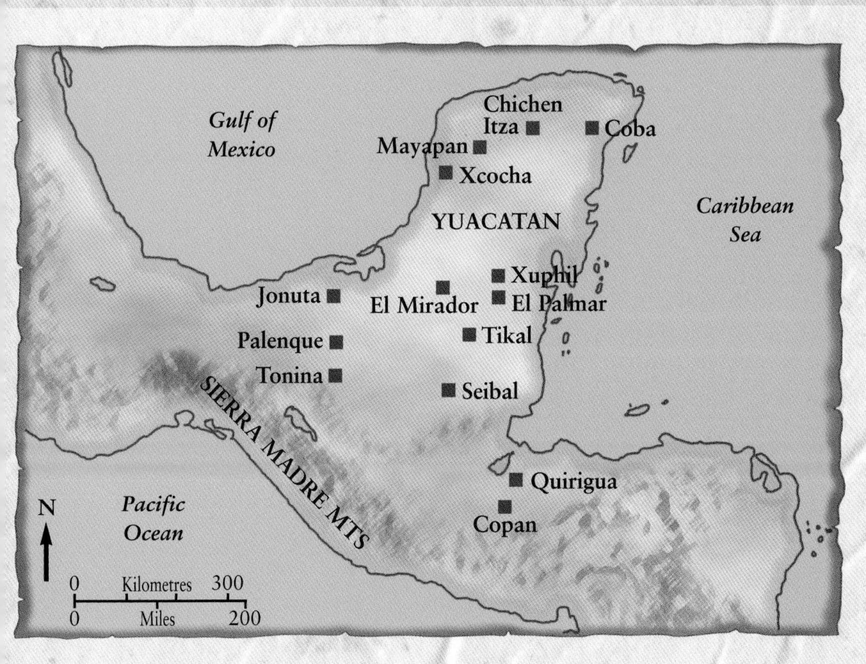

◀ THE MAYA
The Maya came from the Yucatan, the large peninsula that sticks out from the eastern coast of Mexico. They built most of their cities here and in the area to the southeast, now part of Guatemala and Honduras.

Key Dates

- 300BC–AD300 Many of the Maya cities are founded.
- AD300–800 "Classic" phase of Maya civilization flourishes.
- AD900 Most Maya cities are in decline.
- AD900–1200 Cities in the northern Yucatan flourish under the warlike Toltecs, from Tula.

Glossary

Hittite chariot

A

amphitheatre A circular or oval open-air theatre, with seats arranged around a central area.

aqueduct A manmade channel to supply water.

archaeology The study of the remains of past societies. Archaeologists excavate, or dig, in the ground, or search underwater, for buildings, tools, pots, bones and any other objects that provide evidence of how people have lived.

B

Bantu The name given to a large group of African languages, and the people who speak them. The word *bantu* means "people".

bronze An alloy, or mixture, of copper and tin. Bronze is renowned for its strength and durability.

Egyptian mummies

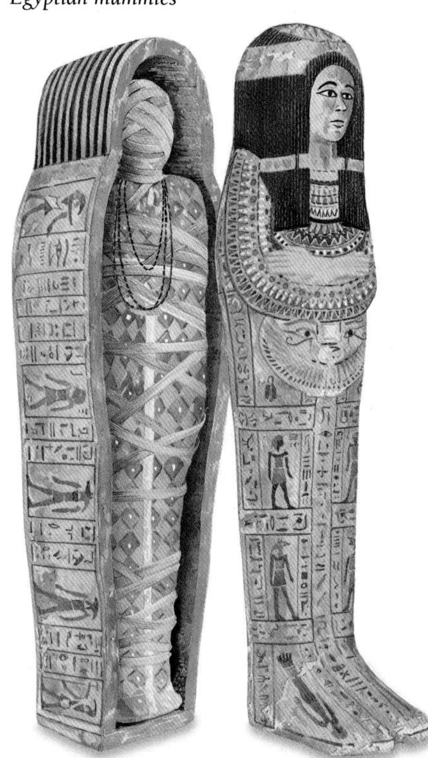

C

caravan A group of people, usually riding camels, who travel across the desert. In the ancient world, Arab and other merchants moved about in this way.

citadel An elevated fortress, which protects a city.

citizen A free man or woman who has the right to vote.

city-state A city that is also an independent state, or country.

civilization A settled society that has developed writing, organized religion, trade, grand buildings and a form of government.

consul One of the elected officials of the Roman republic.

culture This refers to art, literature, music and painting. But it can also be used to describe the way of life of a particular society.

cuneiform A type of writing that uses wedge-shaped figures, carved with a special tool. It developed in Mesopotamia from about 3000BC.

D

dynasty A ruling family.

E

empire A large area made up of different lands or countries, ruled over by one government or leader.

F

fertile Rich or fruitful. Fertile land produces good crops. The earliest civilizations began in an area known as the Fertile Crescent in ancient Mesopotamia.

flood plain Area around a river that is covered by water when the river floods. The soil is usually very rich and fertile.

G

grave goods Items such as jewels, tools or weapons that ancient peoples placed in tombs.

H

hieroglyphics A type of writing used in ancient Egypt that uses pictures known as hieroglyphs.

I

irrigation Using manmade channels or watercourses to bring water to dry land so that crops can grow.

Chinese bronze vessel

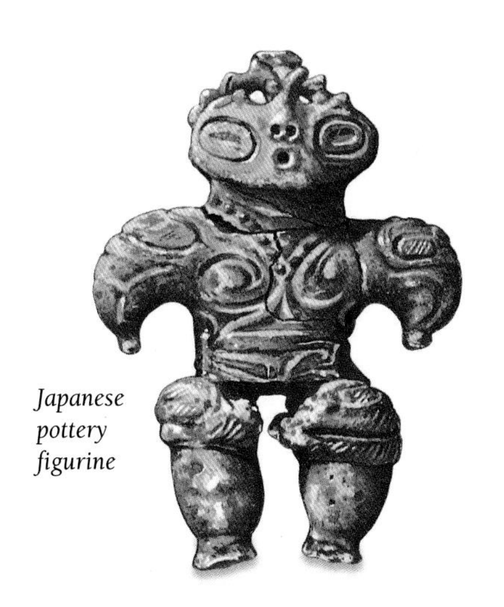
Japanese pottery figurine

K
kiln A furnace or oven in which pottery is fired or baked.

L
legends Stories that are often told about real people or events.

M
Mesopotamia The land between the Tigris and Euphrates rivers. The word literally means "the land between two rivers".

mosaic A picture made from many pieces of brightly dyed stone or glass set into a floor, wall or ceiling.

mummy A mummified or preserved dead body like those of ancient Egypt.

myths Stories told by ancient peoples. Myths often describe the activities of gods and goddesses and were frequently used to explain natural events such as thunder.

O
obelisk A tall, four-sided tapering pillar, usually made of stone, with a pyramid-shaped top.

oracle A means by which ancient peoples could contact the gods to ask for advice or find out about the future. An oracle could be a place, or, as in the case of the Delphic Oracle, a person.

P
papyrus A kind of paper made from layers of papyrus reeds.

pharaoh A title for the later kings of ancient Egypt. The word pharaoh means "great house".

philosophy The study of existence and the meaning of life. Western philosophy began in ancient Greece around 600BC. The word means "love of wisdom".

R
relief A carving that stands out or is raised from the surface.

republic A country or state, such as ancient Rome, ruled by elected representatives of its people.

S
Seven Wonders A list of seven magnificent structures found in the ancient world. They include the Hanging Gardens of Babylon and the Great Pyramid at Giza in Egypt.

shrine A sacred place or container where religious objects or images may be kept.

Silk Road The ancient overland trading route between China and Europe, used mainly by merchants.

Artemis, Greek goddess

T
terracotta Unglazed pottery, usually of a reddish-brown hue.

trade The process of buying and selling goods.

tribute Gifts usually brought by conquered peoples to a ruler.

Z
ziggurat A pyramid-shaped temple built by the ancient Babylonians.

Etruscan palace

Index